BRAVE
STRONG
& *Tender*

Thanks Jim for fathering me in the faith. I saw Jesus Christ wrapped around a faithful servant, husband, father, doctor and laborn which was and still is a tremendous model! Thanks for teaching, helping, encouraging and showing me the way.

You gave your life to me, Bob and

so many others who have gone on do reach and disciple people around the world — that's the fruit of your life!

I will always appreciate how you shared your struggles and failures and then took me to the scriptures and to Him in prayer. Had you been "perfect," I wouldn't have continued to me with you.

Thanks for sharing yourself with me, Suzy and our family. & may we will represent you and the Lord faithfully.

In Christ's love, your spiritual son, Phil

July 16, 1997

BRAVE STRONG & *Tender*

IN EVERYDAY SPIRITUAL BATTLES

PHIL DOWNER

WITH CHIP MacGREGOR

VISION™ HOUSE
PUBLISHING, INC.

GRESHAM, OREGON 97030

This book is dedicated to my three sons:
Paul, Matthew, and Joshua;

And to the three young men for whom I've been praying
daily, who may one day marry my three daughters:
Abigail, Anna, and Susanna;

And to the men and women throughout the United States
who are committed to the ministry of evangelism and
discipleship through CBMC, to which all the royalties
derived from the sale of this book will be contributed.

—*Phil Downer*

CONTENTS

SECTION III
THE SOLDIER AS SERVANT

ACKNOWLEDGEMENTS

I would like to thank the people who built into Susy's and my life as our disciplers and mentors, including Jim and Mary Gail Lyon, Liane Day, Dave and Judy Hill, and Joe and Gladys Coggeshall, through whose lives God worked to bring us to Himself and teach us to walk with Him to reach others for Christ.

What a tremendous blessing I have received from the godly and inspirational leadership of the Board of Directors of CBMC, and the sacrificial service of the staff, members, and friends, faithfully serving throughout the United States in the cause of winning and discipling business and professional men, their wives, and their families. Our vision statement is: Compelled by Christ's love—empowered by God's Spirit. We impact the world by saturating the business and professional community with the gospel of Jesus Christ by establishing, equipping, and mobilizing teams where we work and live that yield spiritual reproducers. "One shall become a thousand" (Isaiah 60:22).

Great thanks is due the entire Vision House staff, including John and David Van Diest. I especially want to thank Chip MacGregor, my dear friend, co-laborer, and fellow soldier, who suffered through, wrote, edited, and rewrote this lawyer's wordy, hyper-detailed, and sometimes meandering text. Thank you, Chip, for your genius. Without your patience, diligence, and expertise, the writing of this book would not have been possible.

Last, and most importantly, I want to thank Susy, my wife of twenty-five years, who is my closest friend, partner, and confidant in our mission to be wholeheartedly devoted to making disciples.

CHAPTER ONE

The Christian Soldier

The call came at midnight. "Phil," the voice said, "something's up. Can you help me?"

I recognized the voice. He was a successful businessman, a guy who rarely asked anyone for help because he thought he could tackle any problem by himself.

"Sure, Tom," I said. "What's up?"

"Janet's leaving me."

I sat down in the dark. *Here we go again*, I thought to myself as Tom poured out his heart in pain. It seems I keep running into the same issues. I keep meeting Christian men who have worked for years to build a strong business, only to watch a weak marriage crumble. The Lord keeps bringing into my path Christian men who have slipped into sexual sin because they thought no one was looking, or guys who can't seem to find fulfillment in life, even though they have every material thing they could ever want. I know the feeling.

After serving in the Marine Corps in Viet Nam, I became a successful trial lawyer. I worked on many of the cutting-edge cases across the country from my office in Atlanta. I had a great law practice, a beautiful wife, and a place in the social echelon. At the same time, I was desperate for God. I didn't get along with people. I had destroyed my marriage and I didn't even know it. I had become an elder in my church simply to show everyone what an upstanding guy I was. And for some reason, my life wasn't the smashing success I had made it out to be.

Then, one day, some friends invited me to a luncheon where a businessman shared Christ. Several months later I came to Christ and a man began discipling me. At first, I knew that I had peace with God, and I felt content knowing that all my past sins were forgiven. Then I began experiencing some rather hard things. I realized that I had to rebuild my relationship with my wife. I had to fight off the temptations toward selfishness and pleasure-seeking. I started to notice that other people were hurting and needed help. Suddenly, I felt like I was back in the Marines, fighting in a battle. Of course, I was, but I never understood that before. That's when my life started to change. If I was going to be in a battle, I knew I had to prepare for it.

Are You in the Battle?

Often, as I have an opportunity to speak to groups, I ask the question, "How many of you feel like you're in a battle?"

It's usually the men who raise their hands. Being a Christian in this world means you're in combat. And it's going to require strength and self-control to win. So I began the process of developing myself into a Christian soldier. Eventually, I found that my attitude toward my work had changed. Rather than struggling to make a name for myself so that I could make more money, I began seeing my job as a vehicle for spreading the hope and love found in Jesus Christ. Then, my relationship with my wife changed. Instead of using her and loving things, I began to love her and use things. Even my attitudes toward other people changed. I no longer viewed people as the enemy. Fourteen years later, the Lord told me that He wanted to use me someplace else in the battle. Now I'm the president of Christian Business Men's Committee of the USA, and I often see my former life played out in the lives of many others.

Our society is filled with Christian men who don't understand that they're in a war. They think the Christian life is about meetings and creating an image rather than leading and developing holiness. They may talk about being in the army of the Lord, but they have no idea how to fight in a battle. I see guys who can give a great testimony at the prayer breakfast, but who can't seem to live out their faith daily. I see men who aren't fornicating, but they treat strangers better than they treat their wives. These guys aren't beating their kids, but their sons have to schedule appointments to see them. They're about twelve steps away from a fulfilled Christian life. They *know* the faith, but they can't *do* the faith.

Nothing drives men today like success, and since culture has defined success as attaining wealth, fame, and rank, Christians are also out pursuing those things. That's created a generation of men who are married to their careers—men who are unwilling to say "no" to their bosses, or "enough!" to their businesses; men unable or unwilling to view their jobs as strategic positions in the battle to reach others with the love of

Christ; men so afraid of not having money that they've become slaves to their positions, paralyzed at the thought of losing anything. I routinely see men so wrapped up in the pressures of this life that they no longer have any emotional energy left for anyone else. Not only are they not loving their wives, they don't have a spirit of love for their families. They aren't even focused on the right things—they spend their time worrying about sports, or money, or the Internal Revenue Service, while ignoring their kids and their co-workers who are lost and on the path to hell.

I suppose most men live this way because that's what they saw in their fathers. We learn how to be men from watching Dad, and too many men live in the shadow of an ugly dad. I see men whom Christ has called to be leaders who can't lead because they never learned how. As boys, they always held the dumb end of the tape measure when their fathers were building something. Dad couldn't be bothered explaining what he was doing. So the son never learned to teach, he doesn't know how to model service, and he won't admit his weaknesses for fear that others will find out what he's really like. Maybe his father never once said, "I'm sorry," so he won't either. That lack of humility limits a man's ability to develop relationships. Those are the guys I want to reach out to. Those are the men I want to help grow in their walk with Jesus Christ. Faithful men have helped me, and I want to help others in return.

So as I sat on the floor in the dark that night, listening to Tom's phone call, I wasn't in a state of shock. More than anything else, I felt disappointment that another key guy had wiped out. It turned out that he had recently bought a new phone answering machine. In setting it up he hadn't followed the directions properly, so it had recorded his rather lusty telephone call to a female co-worker. His wife had played the tape, thinking it was a simple phone message, then packed a bag and left him. He thought it was all the fault of the recording machine rather than his total lack of integrity in his marriage. My question for him was simple: "Who do you think you're hiding from?"

Preparing for Battle

For some reason, we seem to have talked ourselves into the notion that Christians can co-exist with this world, that we don't have to be terribly different, just sort of polished up. That leads people to think they can get away with sin, since everybody else is doing it. That's nonsense. Jesus called His disciples to be radically different, and He expected them to set the world on fire with their difference. He once guaranteed us that "in this world you will have trouble" (John 16:33). The apostle Paul continued that thought by saying, "In fact, everyone who wants to live a godly life in Christ Jesus will be persecuted" (2 Timothy 3:12). Christians are in a war, a spiritual battle that pits God's people against the spiritual forces of evil in the world. Peter put it this way: "But you are a chosen race, a royal priesthood, a holy nation, a people for God's own possession, that you may proclaim the excellencies of Him who has called you out of darkness into His marvelous light" (1 Peter 2:9). If you aren't in the battle, if your Bible sits on your dresser from Monday through Saturday without being picked up, then you need to get prepared for the fight.

The reason we are losing the moral war in America is because many Christians have forgotten that they are soldiers. We keep giving up ground to the enemy. It used to be that we all agreed abortion was wrong. Now it's being protected as a constitutional right. It used to be that we all agreed drugs were destructive and evil. Now there is a growing call for the legalization of drugs in America. It used to be that pornographers were the bad guys, to be tracked down by the authorities and thrown in jail for flesh-peddling. Now every perversion known to man is paraded under the guise of artistic freedom, and trying to prevent its exposure even to children is considered censorship. The prophet Isaiah, in describing a perverse culture, warned, "Woe to those who call evil good and good evil, who put darkness for light and light for darkness, who put bitter for sweet and sweet for bitter" (Isaiah 5:20). At the end of the twentieth century we are experiencing a battle over the debasement of culture, and the Christian is called to be a soldier in the battle, reaching people for Jesus Christ and letting Him change them.

A Christian soldier has to be a leader. He needs to know the qualities necessary to take others into battle. The fact is, I wouldn't be a soldier if someone had not taken the time to disciple me. A team of men have poured their lives into mine. I needed some guys who smelled of battle to lead me by the hand and help me learn how to fight as a Christian soldier. As a believer, you've got people looking at you, to see how you'll respond in a culture desperate for integrity and godliness. Let them in on your struggle. Lead them to maturity in Jesus Christ. Without leaders, the war is lost.

A Christian soldier has to be an example. He's got to know what his role is, what the objectives are in the battle, and how to successfully achieve them. During the Viet Nam War, I found that the war-weary soldiers were always treated with respect in camp. Everybody in the Marines knew that the guys in the trenches were the ones who would win or lose the war, that they set the example. The Bible is clear on the things a man is to be: "above reproach, the husband of one wife, temperate, self-controlled, respectable, hospitable, able to teach, not addicted to wine, or pugnacious, but gentle, uncontentious, free from the love of money. He must be one who manages his own household well, keeping his children under control with all dignity" (1 Timothy 3:2-4). You see, people are following you. Your children, your spouse, your co-workers, your neighbors—they're all following your lead, and too many men aren't walking the right trail. Part of your task is to set an example for people to follow, and that will mean living a radically different life from those around you.

Becoming Strong in the Lord

When I was in Viet Nam, occasionally somebody would send up a case of beer for the foot soldiers to drink. We never complained about warm beer. We were happy to get anything at all. Yet in our easy-chair Christianity, you can often hear believers complain because the job starts to get tough. Sometimes I'll feel sorry for myself and focus on me instead of on Him. Who ever heard of a battle without wounds? The enemy certainly is trying to inflict pain and suffering in your life. Satan knows there is a battle going on! Sometimes Christians will complain simply because the war is inconvenient. They'll walk out of church whining that the sermon offered "nothing new." But the fact is, soldiers in battle are happy to get any kind of refreshment. A Christian soldier appreciates any time spent in the presence of God, because he understands the importance of regular communication with his Commanding Officer.

I was chatting recently with a young pastor whose board spent an entire evening arguing over where to locate the communion table. "Our church is a lighthouse to a community headed straight toward hell," he told me, "and these people want to fight about where to put the furniture." He understands the principle that a Christian is a soldier. Soldiers don't get worried about civilian matters; they simply want to accomplish their task.

The Christian soldier is also a servant. He knows that to win the war, you've got to win the people. Occasionally I'll meet a Christian who seems to think the battle we fight is with people. It's not. "Our struggle is not against flesh and blood, but against the rulers, against the powers, against the world forces of this darkness, against the spiritual forces of wickedness in the heavenly places" (Ephesians 6:12). People aren't the problem. As a matter of fact, Christ is calling you to love people. We can't win the war without changing the hearts of people. If you're going to be a soldier for Christ, you're going to have to learn to love and serve others—even unlovable people.

I was discussing a newscast with a friend the other day, in which a liberal lawyer had bashed every cause we Christians hold dear. My friend began to criticize her, until I told him, "That's me, twenty years ago." I was in captivity to the enemy, fighting against the things of God. And you couldn't change my mind with pickets or angry letters. What changed me was the love of Christ, expressed through some mature men of God. A couple years ago we watched Jane Roe turn to Christ. She was the plaintiff in "Roe vs. Wade" case, which legalized abortion in America. She wasn't won to Jesus by arguments but by a relationship. Her heart was totally changed by the Lord because His servants were willing to share love rather than simply sharing information. We won't win the war without changing the hearts of people. In fact, that is the war—to go into the world and make disciples (Matthew 28:19).

The apostle Paul, writing to the Christian believers in Ephesus, told them to "be strong in the Lord and in his mighty power. Put on the full armor of God so that you can take your stand against the devil's schemes…. Therefore take up the full armor of God, that you may be able to resist in the evil day, and having done everything, to stand firm" (Ephesians 6:10-13). Paul had already spent several chapters talking about the Christian's identity and character. We have been adopted, loved, forgiven, enlightened, and empowered. We have been removed from the dominion of Satan and positioned in the kingdom of Christ. We have been delivered out of our old lifestyle, into a new life with the Lord. The way we think, talk, and act are to be completely changed. Now we are to walk in a manner worthy of the calling we have received—walking in love, in light, in unity, and in the Spirit's wisdom. Our relationships, our marriages, our families, our employment, even our songs are to be changed. But amidst all this change, Paul wants us to know that there will be a battle. We can't take victory for granted. Just because you've been told how to treat your family doesn't mean you will automatically do it that way. Even though you know how you should approach your work that doesn't mean you'll pull it off. Just because you know the truth doesn't mean you will apply it. God's power is available to heal your marriage, but the enemy wants to thwart the Lord's work in your life. Paul called the conflict between pursuing the active Christian life and the devil's schemes to hinder it a "war," and you are in the middle of it.

Remember, Jesus' ministry began with a battle against Satan. After the Lord had fasted for forty days, Satan came and tempted Him to compromise (see Matthew 4:1-11). That spiritual war continued to rage for the next three years. At the end of His earthly ministry, Jesus sweat great drops of blood because of the intensity of the battle. Whether you're at the beginning or the end of your Christian walk, you are part of the battle. It doesn't get any easier over time, either. As it was for Christ, you'll find that the Christian life gets harder the more mature you get. Satan works overtime to keep you from being strong and effective in walking with Christ and reaching others for Him. The Christian life never stops being a war, and the enemy is hell-bent on your destruction. Christ has won us for eternity, but the enemy wants to destroy our marriages, our families, our businesses, and our ministries in the lives of others.

Sometimes the battle is physical. Jesus had to endure the cursing, punching, and spitting of His accusers, culminating in the nailing of His hands and feet to the cross. The apostles endured physical pain and eventual martyrdom for the cause of Christ. But more often the battle is supernatural, where Satan uses others as pawns to attack us for our faith. Although defeated by the cross, he is a strong, subtle, and clever enemy on earth, and he has one goal for Christians—to destroy them. We are not just the sons of God; we are His soldiers. And "the weapons we fight with are not the weapons of the world. On the contrary, they have divine power to demolish strongholds. We have the authority to demolish arguments and every pretension that sets itself up against the knowledge of God, and to take captive every thought to make it obedient to Christ" (2 Corinthians 10:4-5). It's certainly possible to become weary in the battle, but the more you fight, the greater your string of victories becomes. And the more victories you experience, the greater your confidence in God. Your victory is in Him. I've always appreciated Paul's words to the Corinthians about remaining in Ephesus so that he can fight the battle: "I will stay on at Ephesus until Pentecost, because a great door for effective work has opened to me, and there are many who oppose me" (1 Corinthians 16:8-9). I've met plenty of people who talked about getting out of their jobs, businesses, or ministries because things were too difficult, but Paul reminds us that that he stayed in simply because he knew there was a battle to fight. And he wanted to finish fighting the good fight.

So consider Paul's commands to the believers at Ephesus who were getting ready to go to battle. "Be strong in the Lord and in his mighty power," he writes in Ephesians 6:10. In other words, be prepared to go into battle. Find your strength in Jesus Christ. No matter how strong our enemy is, Christ's strength is greater. As the apostle John put it, "The one who is in you is greater than the one who is in the world" (1 John 4:4). I have come to believe that the smallest amount of divine power can overcome the greatest of evil. God's strength is in you. According to Philippians 4:13, "I can do everything through Him who gives me strength." You see, Christ dealt a death blow to Satan at the cross. The devil thought he had finally defeated God, but "through death He destroyed him who holds the power of death—that is, the devil" (Hebrews 2:14). So if Christ has already defeated Satan, and if you are in Christ, then you have also defeated him. And since Satan is subject to Christ, he must also be subject to Christ in you. The devil is a vanquished foe; he has no strength to withstand the resurrection power that exists in every believer. You no longer have to be afraid in battle!

The Example of Timothy

When Timothy was a young man in ministry, he was fearful. No doubt Timothy was tempted by the same lusts and pride every young man faces. He was also under attack by people trying to propagate false doctrine. As a result, he began to have doubts. He might even have become timid and ashamed of the gospel he was preaching. So his spiritual father, Paul, wrote to remind him of the battle. "Be strong in the grace that is in Christ Jesus," Paul says in 2 Timothy 2:1. "Endure hardship like a good soldier of Jesus Christ." He also reminded Timothy that "God has not given us a spirit of timidity, but a spirit of power, of love, and of self-discipline" (2 Timothy 1:7). Don't fool yourself into thinking you have lost the spiritual battle. God has the resources you need for victory. He has shared His great power with believers—power that conquered death, power that exalted Christ, and power that defeated Satan.

Your strength is found in Christ, not in yourself. Paul once told a group of Christians, "I pray that the eyes of your heart may be enlightened in order that you may know the hope to which He has called you, the riches of His glorious inheritance in the saints, and His incomparably great power for us who believe. That power is like the working of His mighty strength, which He exerted in Christ when He raised Him from the dead and seated Him at His right hand in the heavenly realms, far above all rule and authority, power and dominion, and every title that can be given, not only in the present age but also in the age to come" (Ephesians 1:18-21). Christ has great power, and He has made that power accessible to all believers.

Of course, we still sin—often when we think we're immune to temptation. That's why 1 Corinthians 10:12 warns, "If you think you are standing firm, be careful that you don't fall!" But when you depend upon God, there is nothing Satan can do to defeat you. As a matter of fact, His strength is most available to you when you are weakest: "My grace is sufficient for you, for my power is made perfect in weakness...for when I am weak, then I am strong" (2 Corinthians 12:9, 10). There is no reason to feel defeated. As the Lord said to King Jehoshaphat, "The battle is not yours, but God's" (2 Chronicles 20:15).

In Ephesians 6, Paul wants Christians to take seriously the concept of spiritual warfare. We have direction and power from God, but it still is not easy. The Christian life is warfare, and every believer is a soldier. Satan and his demons are hard at work trying to disrupt your relationship with God and your reaching out to others in love. They'll use persecution and peer pressure to get you to compromise. They'll try to undermine God's character and the credibility of Scripture. They'll attempt to confuse you with false doctrine, bring division to the body of Christ, separate you from those who need Him, and do all they can to hinder your service to the Lord. More than anything else, they will put things in your way to make you comfortable in this world or feel hypocritical about your faith and your life. If they can get you to believe your faith doesn't make you any different, they have co-opted the power of God in your life.

When you live your life for Christ—loving your wife as Christ loved the church, having a biblical attitude toward your work, nurturing your kids in the ways of the Lord, and reaching out in love to others with the gospel—you will be confronting the world and its systems. Too many Christians have been willing to accommodate the world, believing they can win everyone to Christ by becoming like the world. That's dead wrong. We'll win people by living like Christ and sharing His truth and love in this world. Unfortunately, you'll also find that people hate you when you do that. They hated Christ when He came, because they couldn't live with His perfection. That's why Jesus said, "If the world hates you, keep in mind that it hated me first. If you belonged to the world, it would love you as its own. As it is, you do not belong to the world, but I have chosen you out of the world. That is why the world hates you....If they persecuted me, they will persecute you also....They will treat you this way because of my name, for they do not know the One who sent me" (John 15:18-21).

Becoming a Soldier

Christian, it's time to put on the full armor of God. Make sure your loins are girded with truthfulness—the truth will protect your changeable feelings. Put on the breastplate of righteousness, to guard your heart. Strap on the helmet of salvation, so that you're certain in your mind that you are saved. In your hands pick up the shield of faith, to protect you from the enemy's attacks, and the sword of the Spirit, to go on the offensive in the battle. And start to "pray in the Spirit on all occasions with all kinds of prayers and requests. With this in mind, be alert and always keep on praying for all the saints" (Ephesians 6:18). Armor is required for every soldier going into battle. Put it on now, so you'll be prepared for the war.

If you are willing to fight the battle and pay the price for victory, God will give you victory beyond anything you've ever known. Imagine the thrill of hearing Him say upon your arrival at your true home, "Well done, good and faithful servant," and the voices of many saying, "I'm here because Christ reached me through your life." The greatest joys come from the greatest battles. Our churches are full of people who don't understand that this life is a war, filled with battles each day. We need people trained to fight. We need some winners— some Christian soldiers to serve, to model, and to lead. You only have one chance at this life. When you fire your last shot, you want to go out a victor. This book is designed to help you know how to become a victorious soldier in the army of God.

The Soldier as Leader

SECTION ONE

CHAPTER TWO

How to be Strong

I have a friend who used to work with the circus. One of the features was "Gent, the Strong Man." Gent could tear a phone book in half, bend steel bars, and bite nails in two. He demonstrated incredible feats of strength, beyond what most of us could imagine. But according to my friend, Gent was a wimp in many other ways. He couldn't make up his mind about anything, was insecure about the value of his act, and had no confidence in dealing with other people. He was also easily bullied by his wife, a little bit of a thing who worked in the trapeze act. When she left him for another trapeze performer, Gent turned to the bottle for comfort. For all the posing and flexing of muscles, Gent was nothing but a weakling in life.

It's amazing how we have come to equate physical strength with inner strength. The two often have nothing to do with each other. General Phil Sheridan was just 5'2" and weighed less than 120 pounds, but his grit and mental toughness made him one of the strongest military leaders of the Civil War. A soldier who pumps iron won't necessarily be the best or the strongest soldier, though he may have the biggest biceps. Strength for a soldier means being mentally tough, having the character to resist attack, and being effective and intense during a battle. For the Christian soldier, the ability to allow the strength of God to work through him is imperative.

Timothy was one strong guy. Most people don't see him that way, since he suffered from nerves, had a weak stomach, and was raised by women. In my neighborhood, Timothy probably wouldn't have been singled out as a leader. He was a half-breed, the son of a Jewish mother and a Greek father. His dad wasn't around, so he was raised as a mama's boy in a single-parent household. He was frequently ill, so that his mentor once had to encourage him to "use a little wine because of your stomach and your frequent illnesses" (1 Timothy 5:23). It's interesting that when the apostle Paul first introduced Titus, in 2 Corinthians 7:5-7, he mentioned how the young man had come into the middle of a dangerous conflict and brought comfort and confidence. But when Paul introduced Timothy, he felt it necessary to instruct them about treating the new guy with kid gloves: "If Timothy comes, see to it that he has nothing to fear while he is with you, for he is carrying on the work of the Lord" (1 Corinthians 16:10). Paul had to remind Timothy to be strong. In 2 Timothy 1:7, he wrote, "God did not give us a spirit of timidity, but a spirit of power, of love and of self-discipline."

But Timothy became strong in the Lord. He started out being weak, but he ended up being used greatly by the Lord. He served with Paul in Philippi, Caesarea, Corinth, Berea, Ephesus, and Rome. He went to prison for the cause of Christ. He walked with God, and received great honor from Paul in his letters.

The apostle once wrote to Timothy and said, "Be strong in the grace that is in Christ Jesus. And the things you have heard me say in the presence of many witnesses entrust to reliable men who will also be qualified to teach others. Endure hardship with us like a good soldier of Christ Jesus. No one serving as a soldier gets involved in civilian affairs—he wants to please his commanding officer. Similarly, if anyone competes as an athlete, he does not receive the victor's crown unless he competes according to the rules. The hardworking farmer should be the first to receive a share of the crops" (2 Timothy 2:1-6). Now that's a man's passage. Paul uses three different images that describe a strong man of God: The soldier, the athlete, and the hardworking farmer. All of them have to work hard. There are no shortcuts to success. A soldier has to spend hours and hours learning to march, knowing how to break down his gun, and understanding the importance of obeying the chain of command. It takes a lot of hard work, and without it he will never be a good soldier. An Olympic athlete will spend years running, training, and doing exercises that will prepare him for his moment in the games. If he slacks off his training regimen or tries to bend the rules, he won't win. A farmer has to get up early and do the work, day in and day out. He can't just take a week off because he's tired, or the crops and animals will die. Being a Christian soldier has to be approached with the same mental attitude as those three tough jobs.

There are no shortcuts to maturity. If you're really serious about your walk with God, you might as well decide right now that it's going to be a lot of hard work. You're going to have to exercise your spiritual muscles. You're going to have to work when you don't feel like working. And you can expect to take some bruises occasionally. I'd like to sugarcoat this for you, but I can't. Those are the facts.

Nobody said being a Christian is an easy job. There is good news, however. Timothy, weakling though he started out to be, became a tough soldier. He discovered that by being weak before God and allowing the Lord's strength to work through him, he had the strength of God at his disposal. He overcame much to become strong in grace, and being strong in grace is significantly different from being strong in the world. The way to do it is to let God be strong through you. You have to admit that you have a number of pressures in your life—marriage, family, work, ministry, a mortgage, aging parents, activities—and you can't handle them all. You can't juggle that many balls. But God can.

You might look at a newspaper and think, "The world is going to hell. My neighbors are going to hell. There is war and strife everywhere, Satan's spokesmen are preaching a false religion, and all Americans can think about is acquiring more toys. On top of this, I've got my family to think of and all these bills to pay. There are too many challenges—I can't do it all!" Funny, but Paul once said almost the very same things. When he was writing to a church that had caused him no end of heartache, he told them, "There was given me a thorn in my flesh, a messenger of Satan, to torment me. Three times I pleaded with the Lord to take it away from me. But He said to me, 'My grace is sufficient for you, for my power is made perfect in weakness.' Therefore I will boast all the more gladly about my weaknesses, so that Christ's power may rest on me. That is why, for Christ's sake I delight in weaknesses, in insults, in hardships, in persecutions, in difficulties. For when I am weak, then I am strong" (2 Corinthians 12:7-10).

I'm glad I don't know what Paul's weakness was—it makes me wonder if his were the same as mine. It does me good to know that Paul was weak. I was never treated like a Timothy, so it's good for me to see how a weakling could be used by God in a mighty way. For a long time I struggled with those words of Paul. I thought God wanted me to be strong. Why would he boast about his weakness? I generally hide mine. Then one day I thought about the ministry of Timothy. If an unbeliever looked at the work of Paul, that individual might have a tendency to chalk up Paul's success to his great gifts. But when that same unbeliever examined the ministry of Timothy, he would have to come to the conclusion that God was at work in Timothy's life. You see, God shows His greatness by using weaklings to accomplish mighty works. His power is made perfect in our weaknesses, so perhaps He does His greatest work when we completely empty ourselves before Him.

For example, I have a lot of experience speaking. That's a strength of mine. Sometimes when I know I've got a great message, I have a tendency to just go out and let it happen. There's no need for me to pray; I can rely on my own strength to communicate to the audience. On the other hand, when I'm struggling over what to say, I have a tendency to spend considerably more time in prayer, asking the Lord to use me in spite of my weakness. But I think God wants me to rely upon Him whether I'm ready or not. He wants me to spend time in prayer asking Him to speak through me even when I feel I've got everything down pat. That allows God to get the glory. It helps everyone to see His power at work in me. That's when I can be strong in God's grace.

Most men have a tough time admitting they have weaknesses. Much of our culture is built around trying to hide any weakness. That is why it's such a joy to have developed over the years a team of men to whom I can admit my weaknesses, get prayer, and find encouragement and help. Men are filled with fears in our culture. They're afraid of closeness, afraid of hypocrisy, afraid of poverty, afraid of competition, afraid of emotion, afraid of intimacy, and afraid of making a mistake. But God didn't give us a spirit of timidity! He wants us to be strong men, unafraid of being emotionally close to our wives, our friends, our children, and the guys we are discipling. He wants us, like Paul, to delight in our weaknesses, so that we can see the strength of God at work. A man afraid is a man in bondage. I've met men who can put together multi-million dollar deals, but who are afraid of talking to their co-workers about a bad marriage. They're in bondage to the image they have of what a man should be. This bondage makes them weak.

God wants us to be strong, but His idea of strength is that we rely completely upon Him. The more we rely upon Him, the stronger we become. It's interesting, but a woman's definition of strength is probably much closer to God's than a man's is. Men have a tendency to think of strength as being connected to physical or natural ability. Usually, a woman's idea of a strong man is someone who can reveal himself. Before you dismiss that idea as someone who's a wimp, think about God's grace being made evident in your weakness. The Lord wants you to use your ability, but He also wants you to learn to rely on Him. He wants you to be close to Him. Real strength is found in preparing your mind for the spiritual battle so that you feel confident, knowing God's Word so that you can fight effectively in the battle, and having the strength of character to resist Satan's attacks and temptations. You get close to the Lord, so that you know His mind, and you admit your weaknesses so that you can rely on His strength in your life.

God also wants strong women in His army, something that the church has had a tough time trying to define. Our culture has made women believe they're getting a bad rap in the Christian church because of all the talk about submission. But it takes great strength to wait on the Lord, to submit yet not surrender your holiness. There are really only two kinds of wives. First, there is the kind who says, "I'll do it my way." There's no waiting on the Lord or waiting for the husband. She's tired of being bullied and tired of waiting for him to take leadership. She meets him in two places: Church and bed. Other than that, she runs her own life. She thinks that makes her strong, but it only makes her isolated—separated from the leadership of her husband and the Lord.

The other kind of wife says, "I'll give in." That's a tremendous sacrifice, and can only be done by a person of strong character, willing to accept God's timing while still holding to her convictions. The influence of a strong woman is incredible. A friend of mine married a widower with grown children. Those kids didn't respect her and didn't want anything to do with her. But she won them over by living like Jesus Christ. Now she is their closest confidant. In a sense, she became like Christ to those kids, and now she has great influence in their lives.

Men, you are called to be strong and live like Jesus Christ. As a strong soldier, you'll be the leader to those around you. To do so, you will have to get involved in what God is doing in our world. You'll need to be discipling others into maturity. You'll need to be discipling your children. This world won't be turned around by politics or principles, but by strong soldiers who can lead others to Jesus Christ.

If you want to develop strength in God, there are four things you're going to have to do. First, you have to acknowledge your weaknesses to God. That may sound odd, but before you can truly be strong you'll have to admit you are weak. There are things you can't do. God has far greater power and is responsible for all things in this life. So admit to Him that you are weak, then ask for His strength. Be honest about your areas of sin—He knows about them already! Any recovered alcoholic will tell you that he couldn't begin to be healed until he admitted his weakness. Christians have to take the same approach. God won't force you to act holy, even though He made you holy in Christ. He'll wait for you to admit that you can't beat sin on your own, and that you need His help to defeat sin and develop holiness in your life. Once God is established on the throne of your life, you can become a mighty warrior. As Robert Murray McShane once said, "A holy man is an awesome weapon in the hands of God." To become a strong soldier, the first thing you must do is admit your weakness. Tell the Lord, "I can't get control of my thought life," or "My lack of self-discipline with money has control over me." Acknowledging your weakness is the first step to strength.

The second step is to begin spending time with the Lord each day. Strength in Jesus is drawn from spending time with Him. The disciples weren't made strong by hearing about Jesus, but by spending hours each day in His presence. Paul didn't leap into immediate spiritual strength. He spent years in Antioch, preparing himself for God's call. There are no short-cuts to maturity. Reading all the current popular books won't take the place of reading Scripture. You have to decide to spend a minimum of ten minutes reading your Bible every day, then having some conversation with God through prayer. You will never grow strong without doing this. Every Christian who has impacted his or her world for the cause of Christ has spent extended time in the Word on a regular basis. Every strong believer I know spends time reading and praying with the Lord, and I find that most are also memorizing Scripture on a regular basis. This discipline was tough for me to start, but it has grown in duration and greatly multiplied in effec-tiveness throughout my life. A simple way to begin is to read the Proverb of the day and a couple of Psalms. For years men followed Senate Chaplain Dr. Richard Halvorsen's pattern called "Words of Wisdom." On the first day of the month, they would read Psalms 1 through 5 and Proverbs 1. On the second day they would read Psalms 6 through 10 and Proverbs

2, and so on throughout the month (yes, the day they got to Psalm 119 took a bit longer than usual!). After doing that for a year, they begin to really know the wisdom of Scripture. Walk Thru the Bible's *Daily Walk* has also proven to be helpful for getting people started in regular Bible reading, and the *Renew Your Mind* Bible memory verses from The Navigators have proven invaluable for helping people get started with a Scripture-memory program.

Start by determining in your mind that you will read a few chapters of the Bible each day. Then make some sort of prayer list. Don't make it all requests, either; fill it up with thanksgiving and worship as well. Try to allow a minute or two of silence, so the Lord can speak to you. After all, prayer is a dialogue between you and God, not simply a monologue wherein you lay before the Lord your demands. Many men follow the ACTS pattern: Adoration of God, confession of sin, thanksgiving for blessings, and supplication for requests. Others take one morning to focus on thanksgiving, another to focus on requests, and still another for self-examination. Whichever pattern you follow is fine, as long as you spend time regularly with the Lord. There can be no strength without doing this. If you really struggle to do this on a regular basis, ask a friend to hold you accountable. Do it together, either in person or over the phone, each morning. Get in the habit of spending time in His presence and you'll soon begin to see His strength in your life.

The third step to developing strength is to learn to trust God. This is a bit harder to define, but it means learning to rely on God regardless of circumstances. God has placed you where He wants you, and He is waiting to see if you'll trust Him. Often this means starting your day with the words, "Lord, I don't know what I'm doing, but I'm trusting you to help me today." When you come to the place in your spiritual walk where you know you can't defeat Satan in your own power, that's the point at which God can begin to pour His strength into you. Admit your weakness and ask the Lord to put His supernatural strength to work in your life. I can't overcome temptation without God's strength. I've tried and tried, but I always fail. If I could do it, Christ wouldn't have had to come and die on the cross. But He did, and now His strength is available to be put to work in my life.

Go before Him and say, "Lord, you know that I'm struggling with my self-discipline. I can't seem to overcome my temptation to overeat. But I trust that you are greater than my temptation, and I surrender to your power. Put your strength to work in my life. Let your strength be evident to everyone. I trust that you can tackle this problem in my life." When you learn to rely on God's strength, you begin to become a strong soldier in the battle.

Finally, begin to exercise your spiritual strength. As God makes you strong, look for victory. Seek out ways the Lord wants to use you to help others. The world around you is in dire need of strong, godly leaders, people who can set an example and help grow others into maturity. Begin to exercise the gifts God has given you, and the Lord will use His strength in you.

We all have weaknesses, but we also have the strength of God in which we can glory. As Christians, we can't go into battle whining about the war. As soldiers in the army of God, we must go into the battle reliant upon the strength of God to get us through it. It's time to be strong.

CHAPTER THREE

Take Courage

I 'll never forget what happened when I decided to stop practicing law. I had just announced to my firm that I would be
leaving to become president of the Christian Business Men's
Committee of the USA, and everybody had made a big deal
about my resignation. Then they forgot all about me. I
became a "nobody." That firm, which had grown from four
lawyers to fifty while I was there, suddenly began moving
without me. I know it was unreasonable, but it hurt. If that
wasn't enough, I still had to work on some very difficult cases.
I didn't feel a part of the firm any more, but I still had to be
fruitful.

One case in particular was unusually difficult, and I found myself fighting an uphill battle. Working on that case with me was a young lawyer whom I had mentored. He was doing what he could to help, but my sinking confidence and our lack of a plan kept him on edge, too. One night, as we walked back to our hotel, head down and shoulders slumped, he said to me, "You know, Phil, I'll never forget the times we stopped everything we were doing on a case just so we could study God's Word."

I looked at him. "Uh…what?"

"Oh, you know what I mean. Remember, you were working on that big Danvers case, and one night after dinner we were both pretty stressed out, so you suggested we get out our Bibles and spend some time in His Word."

"That's right," I said to him, a pale light beginning to dawn. "We did, didn't we?"

We walked in silence for awhile, before I spoke again.

"Josh," I said to my young partner, "we're pretty stressed out again."

"Yeah," he agreed glumly.

"Would you like to spend some time in God's Word again?"

His face lit up. "I sure would, Phil!"

Thinking back on that night, I am humbled. Josh and I had been in trouble before and turned to the Lord. What kept me from turning to Him again? Instead of focusing on the Lord, I had chosen to focus on my fear. We won that case, but we also retained and grew in our faith in God.

Do you ever find yourself spending more time thinking about the size of your problems than thinking about the size of your God? Do you feel locked up because of fear? Christian, if you're going to be a soldier, you are going to have to learn to take courage. No soldier lives in fear. He respects his opponent, and he is careful not to leave himself open to attack, but he isn't afraid to fight. You see, fear can keep you from acting. Sometimes in battle a soldier will get trapped in a firefight and simply freeze up. He can't move. His fear keeps him from doing anything, even the most basic act of protecting himself. A soldier in battle who freezes is going to get hurt because he's not putting up a defense.

That's one of the reasons the military spends so much time training soldiers. They put us through live-fire practices, teaching soldiers to lock and load guns under the duress of live ammunition firing overhead. The commanding officers force their soldiers to do the same old routines over and over again, until they can do them in their sleep. There's a reason for that: When the real crisis hits, the soldier won't even have to think. His training will take over. He's done those same actions so many times that he has a confidence in himself which allows him to successfully follow the routine. There's no room for fear, only for obedience. The fear might come later, when he's had a chance to think through what happened to him, but in the midst of the battle he is focused on attacking the enemy, protecting himself, and accomplishing his objectives. That's the thought Paul had in mind when he said, "Be anxious for nothing, but in everything by prayer and supplication with thanksgiving let your requests be made known to God. And the peace of God, which surpasses all comprehension, shall guard your hearts and minds in Christ Jesus" (Philippians 4:6-7).

When Paul encouraged Timothy about God not giving us "a spirit of timidity, but a spirit of power, of love and of self-discipline," he was reminding his young protege not to be fearful. We don't need to fear, for God is in control. Soldiers in God's army who are ready to lead others into the spiritual battle cannot be timid or fearful. They must take courage in the strength of God.

When Joshua was taking the mantle of leadership from Moses, the Lord challenged him to focus on God and His Word: "Be strong and courageous, because you will lead these people to inherit the land I swore to their forefathers to give them. Be strong and very courageous. Be careful to obey all the law my servant Moses gave you; do not turn from it to the right or to the left, that you may be successful wherever you go. Do not let this Book of the Law depart from your mouth; meditate on it day and night, so that you may be careful to do everything written in it. Then you will be prosperous and successful. Have I not commanded you? Be strong and courageous. Do not be terrified; do not be discouraged, for the Lord your God will be with you wherever you go" (Joshua 1:6-9). Those are great words to a great soldier. Joshua, who changed the face of warfare with his military prowess in conquering the Promised Land, had to be courageous if he was going to be a leader. And the Lord instructed him that the way to find courage was to stay in God's Word. Without it, he would have been subject to the paralysis of fear.

There's nothing so scary as a leader paralyzed by fear. During much of the 1930's, when England was led by the weak and vacillating Prime Minister Neville Chamberlain, the United Kingdom was full of fear. The people had no spirit, and a sense of pervading gloom hung over London. His acquiescence to Hitler at the Munich Accords in 1938, ceding much of Europe to Germany, was not only disastrous, but almost treasonous in retrospect. A fearful leader led to a fearful people.

But in May of 1940, Winston Churchill became Prime Minister. In his first speech he promised the people nothing but "blood, sweat, toil, and tears." However, he also told everyone that England was a great country worth fighting for, and they would never surrender to the evil German. He promised to fight not only for England but for the greater cause of freedom. The mood in England turned around overnight. Suddenly there was a spirit that the populace of England could fight the armies of invading Nazis. The courage and determination of Churchill became a symbol for the world's fight against fascism.

Second Samuel 4:1 records what happened when a leader in biblical times lost courage: "When Ish-Bosheth, son of Saul, heard that Abner had died in Hebron, he lost courage, and all Israel became alarmed." If the leader is full of fear, the people will be also. As a soldier in God's army, you are to take courage in the Lord. "Be strong and take heart, all you who hope in the Lord," says the psalmist in Psalm 31:24. The prophet Isaiah was told to "strengthen the feeble hands, steady the knees that give way, and say to those with fearful hearts, 'Be strong, do not fear'" (Isaiah 35:3-4).

God does not want us to be afraid but to trust in His care. When the Jews were rebuilding the temple under Zerubbabel, the Lord sent a message through the prophet Haggai that said, "But now be strong, O Zerubbabel....Be strong, O Joshua son of Jehozadak, the high priest. Be strong, all you people of the land, declares the Lord. And work, for I am with you, declares the Lord Almighty" (Haggai 2:4-5). If we really believe in God as our Commander-in-Chief, we won't fear but we will obey. If you want to drive fear from your life, start spending time in God's Word every day and focus on obeying His commands.

As you develop a love for God, you'll find your fear for the battle disappearing. The apostle John, after reminding us that we are to be God's representatives here on earth, says that, "There is no fear in love, but perfect love drives out fear, because fear has to do with punishment. The man who fears is not made perfect in love" (1 John 4:18). John goes on to say, "This is love for God: to obey His commands" (5:3). When you are loving and obeying God, you have nothing to fear. You can wholly trust that God is in control, and obey Him as He leads you through the battle.

I have found in my own life that when I am full of fear, I am also far from the faith. When I become worried about finances, struggles with ministry, struggles with sin, or any of the thousand other things that can play with my mind, it's usually because I haven't spent my time with God. It happens when I try to solve all the problems by myself, rather than allowing God to work through me. When I start living by what I see, rather than by my faith, I fall into fear. I love Paul's comment to the Corinthian believers that "we are always confident and know that as long as we are at home in the body we are away from the Lord. We live by faith, not by sight. We are confident, I say, and would prefer to be away from the body and at home with the Lord. So we make it our goal to please Him" (2 Corinthians 5:6-9). How many times do we, in the battle, need to be reminded to look to Him rather than at the circumstances?

Peter once learned that lesson. Asleep in a boat at sea, he and the other disciples were awakened in the middle of the night only to see Jesus walking on the water toward them. They were all afraid of the sight, but Jesus said to them, "Take courage! It is I. Don't be afraid." So of course Peter had to try out this new activity. He stepped out of the boat and started walking on the water toward Jesus. "But when he saw the wind, he was afraid and, beginning to sink, cried out, 'Lord, save me!' Immediately Jesus reached out his hand and caught him. 'You of little faith,' he said. 'Why did you doubt?'" (Matthew 14:30-31). As soon as Peter took his eyes off the Lord and started thinking about his circumstances, he began to sink. To be saved, all he had to do was re-focus on Jesus. I find that instructive for my own life.

I was once a man driven by fear and anxiety. I could never please my father, and for some reason I had this image that I had contrived which represented success. My aim was to live up to it, in hopes of finally seeing myself as adequate. I worked hard, driving myself to succeed. My fear ruined my marriage, drove off my friends, and just about cost me my job. In my fear of not pleasing my father, I became just like him, taking out all my tension on my wife. Then some soldiers from CBMC reached out to me and introduced me to the One who could touch my life, forgive my sins, and bring me into an eternal relationship with God. It's amazing, but when I gave my life to Christ, I found I had no more fear. I remember not being afraid, because I was trusting Jesus Christ to take care of everything. Fear still tries to creep into my life now and then. Old habits die hard. I have a tendency to ask myself "what if" questions. "What if the money doesn't come in? What if this doesn't work out?" And as soon as I take my eyes off the Lord and focus on my circumstance, fear returns. But Jesus is there, saying to me, "Have no fear. Look to Me."

There's an old hymn, "Trust and Obey," which some Christians probably look at as rather trite. "Trust and obey," the words say, "for there's no other way to be happy in Jesus." I don't think obeying will automatically make us happy, but I do think it will make us courageous. The great military leader Joshua is famous because of his courage, but that courage grew out of his obedience. Imagine, for example, the day Joshua was told to get two million people ready to cross the Jordan River. There was no bridge, no shallow spot, and no easy way to do it. But rather than haggling with God over the details, Joshua simply trusted that God knew what He was doing, and he obeyed. Scripture tells us that when the first person's foot touched the Jordan, "the water from upstream stopped flowing. It piled up in a heap a great distance away" (Joshua 3:16). I'll bet Joshua's courage grew that day, when he saw that God was going to keep His word!

Joshua had plenty of reason to trust God already, having witnessed the provision of manna, an abundance of quail, and water springing forth from a rock. But those events had happened while Moses, the greatest prophet in the history of Israel, was in charge. Now Joshua was the leader, and he needed to be sure God was going to support him the same way He had supported Moses. So the first test God offered was to cross the Jordan. It didn't make any sense, since there was no logical way to do it. If God had failed to create a way across the Jordan, Joshua would have looked awfully silly. But Joshua was more concerned with obeying God than with his public image. He obeyed, even when it didn't make sense, and that caused him to be a courageous leader. "For the Lord your God dried up the Jordan before you until you had crossed over," Joshua announced to his people. "He did this so that all the peoples of the earth might know that the hand of the Lord is powerful and so that you might always fear the Lord your God" (Joshua 4:23-24).

Soon after crossing the Jordan, Joshua was again called to do something strange. Rather than attacking the city of Jericho, the Jews were to march around it. Every day Jericho had stayed standing. But Joshua was willing to obey the clear direction of the Lord because he trusted God, and on the last time around, the city walls crumbled. His leadership of Israel from that moment on was marked by his courage—a courage that came from a rock-solid trust that God would always keep His word. Joshua attacked Ai even though that city had already defeated Israel once. He attacked the five Amorite kings even though their forces were greater than those of Israel. He set up cities of refuge even though the culture of that time mitigated against such cities. Joshua became a mighty warrior because he knew God would never let him down. Near the end of his life he summed up his courageous faith by warning his people, "Choose for yourselves this day whom you will serve...but as for me and my household, we will serve the Lord" (Joshua 24:15).

Fear can defeat a soldier. It can make us immobile, cause us to forget our task, or even impel us to run from the battle in disgrace. But courage comes when we obey our Commander. It takes courage to obey, but we can never expect to win without obeying.

During the Battle of Cedar Creek in September of 1864, the Union armies had been told the importance of holding the Shenandoah Valley. A strong pre-dawn attack by Confederate soldiers surprised the sleeping Union forces and drove them from their camps. Five-foot, two-inch General Phil Sheridan mounted his great black horse and galloped through his disorganized, retreating men, waving his cap and urging the soldiers to turn and fight. "You've got orders to fight, and fight you will!" he shouted to his troops. The men around him stopped running and began to chant his name. "Damn you," Sheridan continued. "Don't cheer me, fight! Obey my orders and we'll lick them out of their boots!" The Union retreat stopped, they reformed their lines, and they won back the field. The Shenandoah Valley was never again attacked by the Confederacy. Courage, and eventual victory, came by simply obeying orders. The man who had given them knew it would be enough for victory.

When a friend of mine stepped off a helicopter into the war in Viet Nam, his sergeant ordered him to obey every word he said. "Obey me, and you'll live," he was told. Then he was ordered to stow his gear. When he hesitated to look around, the sergeant smashed him in the face, knocking him to the ground. "I told you to obey me. If you stand around like that, you're a prime target for a sniper. If you want to live, next time you'll obey me."

Obedience is the key to courage. If you want to develop courage, you're going to have to learn to obey the Lord. When He calls you to do something, grit your teeth and obey Him. You'll find your courage grows as your obedience allows you to see God bring you victory. Be warned: God may call you to do something difficult. Nobody ever said the Christian life was going to be easy. But as soldiers, we can expect difficult times. The key to getting through them is to be courageous. You might be afraid, but you can take courage in a God who keeps His promises. He won't call you to do anything beyond what you are capable.

I think many men have trouble sharing their fears, even with other soldiers. They think it will make them appear weak. Fear keeps many Christians out of relationships, and it stops others from doing ministry. Think about it: How many times have you not talked to someone about the Lord because of fear? How many people have wanted to accomplish something great for God but have been fearful of trying? Fear puts us in bondage. Faith in Christ frees us from bondage. Christian, you've been given a spirit of power. You can take courage in a great God who is involved in your circumstances and is on your side. If you're going to be a leader in the battle, you need to remain in the Word so that your focus is on the Lord. That's what our world needs today, men and women who don't fear the world but who fear God. As the Lord said in John 16:33, "In this world you will have trouble, but take courage. I have overcome the world!"

CHAPTER FOUR

Developing the Spirit of Power

Who is the most powerful person you know? What makes that person so powerful? Chances are your answer will depend upon your idea of power. Some people confuse power with force, while others believe power comes with recognized authority. The history of mankind is replete with examples of people who lusted for power. They wanted to accomplish great goals, control people's lives, or hold sway over national interests. Some, like Isaac Newton or Michelangelo, used their power to influence people in positive ways. Others, like Joseph Stalin or Caesar Augustus, wielded power almost solely for their own benefit. All of them, whether accomplishing good or evil, shared one similar characteristic: They influenced the lives of people.

Power, at its most basic level, has to do with shaping people. The head of a large manufacturing firm wants to maintain power over his work force, his competition, and his markets. The President of the United States seeks to use his power to influence national and international policy. Most wars have been fought over the issue of power—who will retain it, and who will use force to grab more.

Max Weber, the famous German educator and theorist, claimed that there were several sources of power. *Positional power* is endowed by an organization to an individual, and allows the person limited authority to use power over underlings. For example, the vice president of your company has power over mid-level managers simply because of his position in the organization. He may not be as bright, as informed, or as appealing as any of his staff, but his position affords him a certain amount of power. *Technical power* is that acknowledged by people who admit that another person has specialized knowledge or training beyond their own. Many successful companies are really at the hands of the computer technicians who make everything go. They have no say about products or sales or policies, but without their acknowledged technical skill, everyone else suffers. *Referent power* exists when people within an organization respect the opinion of someone, regardless of their place in the organizational chart. I've seen companies where the word of one long-time salesman is accepted as absolute truth, regardless of what the corporate policy-makers say. Everyone simply recognizes the individual's knowledge and ability, and they trust his word. *Raw power* is simply dominance by brute force. History has shown that raw power is always short-lived, since no one appreciates being forced into subservience.

All of Weber's theories of power are based upon the premise that to have power is to influence the lives of others.

At its essence, that defines power. But if that's the case, our traditional thinking about power is corrupt. Rather than seeking to grab power, we would attempt to influence people so that they came around to our way of thinking. That's what the Lord Jesus did. Rather than coming to earth the first time to set up a kingdom by force, He came and personally shared His love and His vision with twelve men, entrusting them to change the rest of the world after He had left them. With that sort of thinking, the most powerful man is the one who positively influences a few who ultimately influence the lives of many.

An old corporate adage is that if you want to influence hundreds, speak to tens. But if you want to influence thousands, speak to a few. The Lord began His ministry by speaking to huge crowds. Matthew records that great multitudes came to listen to Him preach about values, marriages, and the worries of the day. But as time went on, Jesus spent less time preaching to the many, and more time speaking with the few. By the end of His life, Jesus was spending nearly all of His time with twelve men. One of them betrayed Him and fell away. The other eleven went out and changed the world. That's power.

I always wanted power. I wanted to have a power job, with a power office, and make powerful decisions. I thought that would make me a powerful person, but it only succeeded in separating me from other people. In my heart, I knew that a really powerful person influences others rather than driving them away. Everybody wants that sort of power. Even Stalin wanted to be loved by his people! I believe that interest in shaping others is God-given. Mothers want to nurture their children. Fathers want to mold their boys into strong men. Businessmen desire to mentor others to take their place.

Each of us in our heart of hearts would like to pass on our knowledge and wisdom to someone else. It's part of leaving a legacy. We all seek to leave something behind on earth, to show that our lives have been meaningful. That meaning can never be found in a job, a report, or a building. It's found in people. More than anything, Christians want to influence people, because only God's Word and people's souls will last forever. For all my success as a lawyer, I failed to find that sort of lasting fulfillment until I met Jesus Christ. That's when I finally had something worthwhile to pass along—and more importantly, I finally had a love for others.

Many men, as they age, lie awake nights and ask, "Who'll care if I die?" Sure, a man's wife will shed tears, and a few colleagues will show up to shake their heads at the memorial service. But beyond that, in many cases there will be nothing. That's the fear—that our lives won't count. But a powerful man has influenced the lives of others so that his influence will continue even after he's gone.

What power do we have in Christ? We can't perform miracles, but we all have the power to impact a life for Him. We can all take another person, share the love and the truth of the gospel, and give him the resources to grow into spiritual maturity. We can build into other men and become their spiritual fathers. God has given us the power to be open, loving, and gentle to other people. It doesn't come naturally; admit it, most of us apart from Christ are selfish and not terribly concerned with others until they either get in our way or have something we want. But a Christian soldier who is a powerful leader begins to influence lives for the kingdom.

Paul put it this way: "Though I am free and belong to no man, I make myself a slave to everyone, to win as many as possible. To the Jews I became like a Jew, to win Jews. To those under the law I became like one under the law (though I myself am not under the law), so as to win those under the law. To those not having the law I became like one not having the law (though I am not free from God's law but am under

Christ's law), so as to win those not having the law. To the weak I became weak, to win the weak. I have become all things to all men so that by all possible means I might save some. I do all this for the sake of the gospel, that I may share in its blessings" (1 Corinthians 9:19-23). In other words, Paul, one of the most powerful and influential men of all time, allowed Christ's power to flow through him in whatever way possible so that he could influence those around him for Jesus.

Winning others to Jesus Christ reveals power. It shows that the power of the Spirit is in your life, and it means that God has used you to change a person's life for all eternity. Now that's power. When we can give up ourselves, our positions, and our possessions to assist others, we become powerful leaders in the army of God. After all, what could be more powerful than changing a person for all eternity?

I once spent a year discipling the CEO of a large organization. At first it didn't seem to be doing any good, but after a year I began noticing subtle changes in the man and his attitudes. The casual observer might not have noticed at first, but the way he treated other people had changed. Soon his corporate leadership was following his example. Since he held such an important position in his company, the changes in his life became magnified through his leverage in the organization. When you change a person of influence toward maturity in Christ, you'll find it has a tremendous impact on others. That man's life was changed by the power of God, and it resulted in a significant change in the lives of many people.

I've long been impressed with the power of Barnabas. The first time Barnabas shows up in Scripture is when he wants to help someone else. In Acts 4:36 he sells a piece of property and gives the money to the disciples, to assist the new church in Jerusalem. The next time we see him is in Acts 9:27, when Saul, who had met Jesus on the road to Damascus, was rejected by the other disciples. "But Barnabas took him and brought him to the apostles. He told them how Saul on his journey had seen the Lord and that the Lord had spoken to him, and how in Damascus he had preached fearlessly in the name of Jesus." Saul needed somebody to help him, and Barnabas was there for him.

That sort of behavior influenced those around him, so that it was Barnabas who was chosen by the church in Jerusalem to find out about the hordes turning to Christ in Antioch. The other believers knew they could trust Barnabas to investigate what was happening and give an honest evaluation. It's particularly interesting that Acts 11:25 notes how "Barnabas went to Tarsus to look for Saul" to join him in his ministry in Antioch. Barnabas was a man of power, committed to influencing the life of Paul. In the next chapter Barnabas took on a young man, John Mark, whom he also wanted to mold into maturity. Paul would later split with Barnabas over the unfaithfulness of John Mark, but it's interesting to see Barnabas willing to stand by his protége, even though John Mark had failed them. He still believed in influencing that young man for Christ, and his belief paid off. By the end of Paul's life, he, too, was seeing the value of John Mark, calling him "useful to me in my ministry" (2 Timothy 4:11). Barnabas was powerful not because he had a position of authority, but because everyone around him could recognize his authority through others. He influenced lives for Christ.

The unsaved people around you don't need your information as much as they need your incarnation. They don't need your sagacity as much as they need your Savior. A powerful soldier who wants to be a leader will work at building friendships with non-Christians. You'd be surprised at how many people in our world need a friend.

After speaking at a CBMC luncheon in a major city, I was approached by a well-dressed, prosperous CEO. Looking calm and exuding confidence, success, and stability, he said to me in a very low voice, "Phil, I'm thinking of taking my life. Can you help me?" There was nothing about the tone of his voice or the expression on his face that would have indicated to anyone that we were having a conversation about life and death issues. I agreed to meet with him, and we established a relationship that continued for a period of years, during which time he freed himself from an addiction and received Jesus Christ as his Lord and Savior. None of his friends or work associates had any idea of the crisis he was having, or the feelings of despondency he was experiencing. Truly, men need a friend.

We live a largely isolated, friendless existence. Many people feel relationally disconnected from any other human being. Our emphasis on success isolates us, particularly the expectations we put on men in our society to be insensitive tough guys. If you were to take an interest in another, offering time and concern rather than a sermon, you'd find almost unlimited opportunity for impacting his life, leading him to Christ, and discipling him so that he becomes a disciple-maker. Every individual on earth has what Pascal called a "God-shaped void" in his or her life. You can help fill that void by sharing with him the God he so desperately needs.

You can always spot a powerful leader by how comfortable he is with himself. Most truly great leaders are at ease with their own goals and abilities. Some might be driven to accomplish their tasks, but most are relaxed about themselves. For example, Marv Levy, the longtime coach of the Buffalo Bills football team, is known for being a great coach. Sure, he lost a number of Super Bowls, but the fact that he got his team that far four years in a row is incredible. Whether you like Coach Levy or not, you've got to appreciate how comfortable he is with himself. He's able to laugh at himself, something a lesser man isn't able to do. Laughing at yourself is becoming a lost art in America as men become less sure of who they are. A powerful man is comfortable with who he is, and a powerful Christian is comfortable with who he is in Christ.

I'm friends with a young Christian who was a junior partner in a big law firm in New York. This man was growing in responsibility and influence at his firm. Then one day he came across something his firm was doing that he knew was wrong. He knew it was true, but he couldn't prove it. Yet he stood his ground and spoke out against corruption. The firm turned on him. He was embarrassed, accused, he lost his bonus, and his life was turned upside down. The firm just beat on him in an attempt to shut him up. He wouldn't. He knew his integrity was at stake. He had to stand for what was right. Then it all came to light. He had been right all along, and his whistle-blowing literally saved the firm. Rather than a pariah, that young man became the hero of the day. It takes a powerful man to be able to stand up and state the truth. We all like to think that we live out our convictions, but it takes a powerful man to live out the truth in the face of opposition. You have to be sure of who you are and what you stand for.

If you want to be a powerful soldier for Christ, get to know the truth, then share it with others. In the spiritual war, you can expect to take some hits for standing up for the truth. You can expect to be criticized for sharing your faith. But if we can't handle such little persecution as verbal criticism, we can't expect to ever win the bigger battles ahead. "For it is commendable if a man bears up under the pain of unjust suffering because he is conscious of God. But how is it to your credit if you receive a beating for doing wrong and endure it? But if you suffer for doing good and you endure it, this is commendable before God. To this you were called, because Christ suffered for you, leaving you an example, that you should follow in his steps. He committed no sin, and no deceit was found in his mouth. When they hurled their insults at him, he did not retaliate; when he suffered, he made no threats. Instead, he entrusted himself to him who judges justly" (1 Peter 2:19-23). Sometimes I have to wonder how much "persecution" really happens to most Christians. We think that if a co-worker makes a derogatory comment about our faith, we've suffered greatly. Baloney! Paul receiving thirty-nine lashes was persecution. Your being made fun of at work is simply inconvenient.

If you want to develop a spirit of power, make sure you know what you believe, then start talking with others about it. Start influencing lives for God. Spend enough time in the Word that you know your faith and you've gained God's wisdom. Then share that wisdom with others. You'll find your power growing as you begin molding lives for eternity. You'll also find that as you talk about your walk with Christ, your relationship with Him will deepen. Paul put it this way when he wrote to Philemon: "I pray that you may be active in sharing your faith, so that you will have a full understanding of every good thing we have in Christ" (v. 6). A powerful Christian shares his faith.

Start making an effort to talk with your co-workers. Look for opportunities to chat with the people you see every day. Go out on a limb and ask your neighbors over for dinner— even if you don't have all the home handyman projects completed. That takes courage and power, and it will start you on the path toward sharing your faith.

Of course, it can be lonely doing this by yourself, and CBMC is committed to building teams of couples that can win family, colleagues, and friends to Jesus Christ. We've even developed a video series, *Living Proof*, to train people how to share their faith naturally. The focus is on lifestyle evangelism, and all that most of us have to do is begin looking for opportunities to talk with the people we cross paths with every day.

Power isn't something you gain automatically. It doesn't really come with the job either, which is why so many guys can work for years in an organization and never really influence anyone. Power is granted to those with knowledge and the ability to influence others. As a Christian, you have all the wisdom of the world at your disposal. So if you really want to be powerful, there are two things you must do. First, don't just read the Bible. Begin to study it. Look for the themes and values of Scripture. Explore God's principles and commandments. Examine what the Scriptures have to say about the issues of everyday life. Analyze God's prescriptions for mankind. Compare the wisdom of God to the wisdom of men. Research what the Lord has to say to others in circumstances similar to yours. Consider the life-changing law of God. As you begin to reflect on His Word, you'll find yourself thinking the thoughts of God. "Let heaven fill your thoughts," Paul encourages us. "Whatever is true, whatever is noble, whatever is right, whatever is pure, whatever is lovely, whatever is admirable—if anything is excellent or praiseworthy—think about such things" (Philippians 4:8). As you reflect on the words of Scripture, you'll find yourself with the power of God's wisdom at your disposal.

Second, look for someone with whom you can begin sharing that wisdom. No one is more powerful than the man who influences a life. My co-writer, Chip MacGregor, loves telling the story of Sherwood Anderson, a writer early in this century who mentored Ernest Hemingway, William Faulkner, Thomas Wolfe, and John Steinbeck. Three of his protéges earned the Nobel Prize; four the Pulitzer Prize. Malcolm Cowley, the most quoted American editor and literary critic of all time, called Anderson's influence "incalculable." He once said that Anderson was "the only writer of his generation to leave his mark on the style and vision of the next generation." He was willing to share his wisdom about writing with others, and in the sharing he helped shape the American literary landscape. Imagine what you can do by sharing God's wisdom with others.

God is calling us to be powerful. He doesn't want spineless, impotent soldiers fighting the battle, but wise, powerful soldiers who can use their wisdom for His purposes. He has called you into a relationship with Him so that He can make you powerful. Study His Word, then start using it to influence the lives of others. If you've always wanted to be close to real power, this is your chance.

CHAPTER FIVE

The Loving Leader Part 1

A friend of mine is a successful banker, but he is a failure as a father. The problem is that he has allowed his business to become his baby. All his emotion and energy go toward the success of his business rather than the success of his family. Once, his wife scheduled an appointment with him through his secretary. She showed up at his bank with their two boys. "These are your sons," she said, as if introducing them for the first time. "I thought you should know what they look like." Ouch!

Everybody loves something. A lot of men who develop their entire sense of self through their work love their careers and their businesses. There's nothing wrong with loving your work—I love my work. The problem is that you can't allow your work to take the place of your family. God's Word calls us to love our wives "just as Christ loved the church" (Ephesians 5:25). How did Christ love the church? He loves it sacrificially, caringly, and purely. All of those require work. I usually don't feel like sacrificing. I'd rather think about my own needs than the needs of my wife. And while I want to be caring, often I'm not. Activities and pressures get in the way of my caring for her. Eventually those things can fill up your life to the point that your love for your wife isn't pure. There are too many other things to love. But without love, you can never be a leading soldier.

What does loving have to do with being a soldier? What does it have to do with being a leader? Love is a necessary element for both, and it's one that confuses too many men. Our world is full of guys who aren't leading their families because they're too busy leading their businesses. They love their work more than they love their wives, and it's caused them to fall in the battle. You see, an unhappily married man is going to have a tough time being a strong soldier for Christ. He knows that his weakness at home makes him weak on the battlefield. He's open to attack. He lacks confidence in his ability to help others. Our world is full of men and women in wounded relationships, and a Christian who cannot speak confidently about his relationships is never going to be able to minister to a friend whose marriage is falling apart. If you're going to be an effective soldier, you're going to have to make sure your love-life is in order.

Every Christian is in full-time ministry, and we've all got tremendous pressure in our lives. We all face the challenge of having too much to do. One pitfall of having a heart for ministry is that sometimes men will excuse their inattentiveness to their wives and families because they're involved in ministry.

Reaching out to outsiders becomes an excuse for neglecting our families. I continually remind men in Christian service not to allow their ministry to justify carelessness with their families. Our ministry to outsiders must flow from a deep relationship with our Lord, our wives, and our children if it is to be authentic and life-changing. When men focus on the right priorities, the Lord brings the world to their doorstep to discover what is different.

The fact is, great leaders aren't just known for their administrative ability. They're known for their love. Christ's leadership was marked by His love for us—so much so He was willing to lay down His life on our behalf. The greatest presidents our country has had were known for their love. Abraham Lincoln didn't make war on the South because he hated it, but because he loved his country. Winston Churchill loved England and he loved freedom, so he was willing to lead his people in time of war. Mohandas Gandhi loved India and its people so much that he was willing to suffer pain and imprisonment on their behalf.

In one sense, love has been the difference between the great leaders of history and the evil leaders. Hitler was known more for his hatred of Jews than for his love of anything or anyone. Stalin surrounded himself with hate. Genghis Khan created an entire empire based on hate. But the respected leaders of history have often been marked by love. God is calling us to be leaders, and it will mean becoming men known for our love. Love can tear down societal barriers and bring harmony where there has been discord. It brings meaning to life and distinguishes us as the people of God. When Christ was speaking to His disciples in the upper room, He told them that "all men will know you are my disciples if you love one another." The world wouldn't recognize God's people by their miracles, their preaching, or their clothes, but by their love. When they see real love manifested, even pagans recognize that it comes from God. The apostle John tells us that "God is love" (1 John 4:16), and when people see love they know God is around. Love can make you an effective soldier for Him—one who leads with the needs of others in mind.

Viktor Frankl, the Jewish doctor who survived three years of the Nazi concentration camps, determined that it was love that helped many survive those horrors. As he would work, he would think of his wife. Her smile, her encouraging words, and her wisdom remained with him even though they were separated. Those who had love had a purpose to which they could grab hold. That got them through those dark days. Those who did not have love could not survive, because there was no meaning to their lives. Frankl would later write, "Love is the ultimate and highest goal to which man can aspire."

When I was in the war, I loved the guys in my platoon. Some of them were tough guys to like, but we were bound together and committed to one another. Once, upon being ambushed, we were ordered to evacuate the area. Not one of our guys moved. You see, we had wounded lying in that field, and the Marine Corps doesn't leave anybody behind. Once more we were ordered to leave the area, but we refused to do so until we could take our casualties with us. That love made us better soldiers. Don't make the mistake of thinking that "love" and "toughness" are mutually exclusive. Jesus Christ was one of the toughest guys ever to walk this earth, yet He was known for His love.

I suppose it's impossible to talk about love without mentioning 1 Corinthians 13, the greatest text on love ever written. That passage offers some very concrete principles for developing the love you will need if you are to be a soldier and a leader in God's army.

Love is patient.

I'm not a patient guy. I know what I want to do, when I want to do it, and exactly how I want it to be done. The problem is that people keep getting in my way and preventing everything from going exactly as I planned! Do you ever feel that way? The Bible says that love is patient, and I'm not always sure I know what patience is. I've got my list of things, I'm ready to go, so I don't think I'm being impatient. I'm just being "organized." The trouble is, my organization seems to drive my wife crazy. Rather than taking the time to help other people understand the plan, educate them so they know their part, and assist them so that they succeed, I just expect that everybody will blindly follow what I want to do.

Showing love means that I won't rush through my own plan; instead, I will listen to what somebody else has to say. That takes time. Showing love means that I'll help to make sure everybody knows what we're doing and what his role is in the plan. That takes time. Showing love means that I'll allow one of my kids to fail at a small task so that he learns to accomplish something greater. That takes time.

When I was growing up, my father seldom gave me his time. He was always busy working. When we went on vacation, we did what he wanted to do. There wasn't much input from anyone else regarding our desires for vacation. And if we tried to force our ideas into the plan, we got snapped at. When we were working on a job around the house, he never had time to help me understand what we were doing. I wanted to know how to use a hammer and saw, but my father simply wanted to get the task completed in as little time as possible. So I ended up standing around and being told I was in the way. Sometimes I got to hold the flashlight, or the dumb end of the tape measure, but he didn't have the patience to teach me to use any of the important tools. Rather than helping me to learn and grow, he simply taught me that he didn't have time for me. My dad was a driven, worldly man who didn't have the advantages in life he gave to me, so he did the best he could. I wanted to be different from my dad, but I ended up worse that he was!

When we bought a house in Chattanooga, I was determined that I was not going to make the mistakes my father had made. We needed a fence built on the property, and we turned it into a family project. That was pretty hard for me to do, because I believed I knew what was "right" for that fence. But I was determined to be patient. So I listened to other ideas. Remarkably, the concept improved. I made sure everybody had a role to play, from the smallest to the biggest of our then five children. That took more time, but it brought the family together, which I felt was well worth it.

The task each person received was a little bit of a stretch for him or her, too. Rather than simply giving each child something any dummy could accomplish, I tried to make sure each did a task which caused him or her to learn something. Sure, I could have built it all myself in less time, but I showed my kids how to use the tools. It made for slower work, but I saw the value in helping educate them for the future. That fence took forever, but we ended up with a great fence and some wonderful memories of working together. In addition, I'm not the only one who knows how to swing a hammer now, so the next time there is a handyman project, I can count on somebody else to have the necessary training to do it. Christ has changed me, and I've begun to be a different man from my father.

Patience is a hard lesson for me to learn. It doesn't come naturally. I have to continually pray, "Lord, help me to see how I can be patient. Let the Spirit prod me to work with others rather than to simply insist on my own way." One of the things I learned in the military was that things work best when everybody has a job. A platoon leader can't be scout, machine gunner, radio man, and field director all at the same time. When I have a clear plan, communicate it to everyone, and make sure everybody knows their own part in it, I just get more done. It takes time, but it's worth the effort.

But sometimes I lose focus. While working on the fence one particularly long Saturday afternoon, I made the mistake of setting the goal of finishing one side of the fence to the corner post of our property. Taking my eyes off my purpose of building a team with my kids, and teaching them to work with their hands, I began to bark orders and push my already weary workers. Finally, reaching the post, Paul was using a mechanical wench secured to a tree ten feet away to tighten the 100 feet of six-foot-high uncoiled steel fencing. With each "take up another click" order to Paul, I asked that the fence be further tightened, which gave off a "twang" each time. Paul yelled out, "I think the fence is tight enough," to which I replied in my perfectionism, "No, just one more click." Ignoring his third warning, Paul dutifully gave the wench another tug and suddenly, with a loud "crack," the rope anchoring the wench burst, sending the wench and Paul flying. With a "swoosh" the recoiling fence screamed down the hill and in seconds, an afternoon of work was dashed. Seeing my red face, bulging eyes, clenched jaw, and rigid posture, Abigail, Paul, Matt, and Anna exercised great wisdom and remained silent, probably praying. But Joshua, then 5, who has never lacked in courage said, "Yep, Paul was right. Dad was wrong. It was tight enough!" Humility often comes hard for me.

When the Allied forces planned their invasion of Normandy, they took months going over every small detail of their plan. The planes practiced so they knew exactly what to do. The Navy rehearsed taking troop carriers onto shore under heavy fire. The ground troops practiced where they would go, what it would be like, and how they would take their objective targets. That practice helped them to be patient on D-Day. Working with other people is always hard, particularly if you have a lot of ability. But if you're going to show love, you will have to learn to demonstrate your patience. If you need to develop patience, pray that the Lord will give you a heart for other people. If you can see their needs, desire what is best for them, and suffer while somebody else fails, you'll develop a patient love. Sure, it's tough to be patient when you know exactly what to do. You've got your list and you're ready to start working through it. But if you can develop a heart for people, you'll soon begin to see that your list often has to give way to education or the emotions of those around you.

I took my son Matthew to a rodeo in Gatlin, Tennessee, a while back. We had to stand in lines, move from place to place, and get around to see the various animals and contestants. There were numerous times I would have chosen a shorter line, done things in a different order, or simply made a case for my own way of thinking. But I didn't. I thought it would be better to allow my son to have a day where he got to lead. We had a great time together. At the end of the day my son said to me, "Dad, you're not the most patient father in the world, but I think you're the greatest father." (I think he meant it as a compliment!)

Love is kind.

I remember coming home from work one day to a messy house. There were toys everywhere, clothes strewn about, dirty dishes in the sink, and general chaos reigning. I could feel the anger start to build up inside me. My first inclination was to begin barking commands. The words "Clean this!" and "Put that away!" were right on the tip of my tongue. This family needed somebody to order them around, and I was on the job. Then I saw my wife. She came in, with a look on her face that told me something was wrong, sat down on the couch and said, "Be nice to me."

Now Susy keeps a clean house. She won't stand for the kids just dumping their stuff or neglecting their duties, so I realized that something extraordinary must have taken her away from her responsibilities. I also knew it must have been pretty important or she would never have gone. A woman in a crisis had called and Susy had spent the day ministering to her. So instead of barking commands, I asked her what she'd like me to do to help her. Then I gathered the kids around me and we began attacking the various chores that needed to get done. Rather than focusing on my agenda—"I need a clean house"— I tried to focus on my wife's agenda—"I need a break." And that allowed us to get through the day. It's not the way I preferred to spend my evening, but it's what my wife needed. If you're going to develop a love for people, you're going to have to decide to practice kindness.

I have a friend, a successful businessman, who just blew it with his kids. His business became his life. He never had time for anything except his business, and his kids wound up in trouble, either because of their father's lack of direction in their lives or just as a means of getting attention. His wife threatened to leave him. When we got together to talk, that man realized that he had allowed his business to take the place of his family. I still remember his words to me: "What an unkind thing I've done."

So he decided to put his lifetime work at risk. He left the love for his business and began to invest in love toward his family. He began finding ways to romance his wife and rebuild his relationship with his kids. The key ingredient was kindness —he simply started doing nice things for his kids. He gave them time. He took an interest in their lives. Eventually he cashed out his business, set up a family foundation, and got everyone involved in ministry. He would ask his kids, "Where do you want the money to go?" and then let them decide who they should support. Kindness brought his family back together.

I used to be an unkind person. I didn't have a heart for people, so I couldn't show kindness because I didn't have any love. If my wife came to me with a problem, I'd immediately offer a solution. She didn't need a solution; she needed a caring partner. I had to learn to offer kindness rather than solutions. If a co-worker came into my office with a problem, my response often was, "You created the problem; you have to create the solution." I had to develop a heart for people so that I could show the kindness that would make me a good leader. My desire was to lead them to Christ and to a life of disciple-making, but I couldn't achieve that goal without loving kindness. So I prayed for God to give me a heart for people.

My work put me with unsaved men and women—people who were slaves to sin and didn't know it; individuals were going to spend eternity in hell, separated from God for all time, and my attitude was "Ho-hum; it's no big deal." I needed a heart for people, so I prayed that the Lord would open my eyes to the needs of others. I prayed He would fill my heart with love for those who didn't follow Christ. I asked Him to give me opportunities to display kindness, even though I had always resented having to put somebody else first. I prayed for a long time, and God began to change my heart.

Love is not jealous or envious.

People filled with the love of God aren't filled with jealousy toward others, a concept that has become part of the American psyche. You see, in our dog-eat-dog corporate world, envy reigns. Much of the system is based on getting what somebody else has, and making sure to guard what you've already attained. That's jealousy. Carefully protecting your rights has become part of our culture. You can hardly pick up a newspaper without seeing another story about someone suing over a violation of rights. We've become so "individual rights" conscious that we've forgotten the value of collective sacrifice. Rather than focusing on what will be morally good for our country, we've become a citizenry interested only in what will be best for us as individuals.

At the founding of our country, the people wanted to establish basic rights. They added the first ten amendments to our Constitution, called it "The Bill of Rights," and assured the citizens of America the rights to assembly, free speech, religion, and the like. The purpose of that bill was to protect the individual liberties of a free citizen from a totalitarian government. The framers of the Constitution wanted to make sure that power resided with the people, not the state house. The rights of individuals were to be honored, with the thought that they would in turn honor one another. But in recent years the political landscape of our nation has changed radically, so that now "rights" not specifically identified in the Constitution are being "discovered" by the judicial system, and individuals are more concerned with being able to do anything they want than with having a common morality. That's jealousy, placed on a macro scale.

More and more people seem to think that "freedom" means "license." In other words, they want to be able to do anything that comes into their minds without anyone else interfering. For example, the argument being foisted on us by those who would legalize drugs in this country goes something like this: "This is a free country, so I should be free to do anything I want. If I choose to take drugs and ruin my life, that's my right." That sort of libertarian thinking completely distorts the Constitution, which was based on a shared morality. The argument that one's behavior "will hurt no one else" suggests that the absence of harm makes something acceptable, which is incorrect. The presence of good is more important. So if we as a country decide that drugs are bad because they ruin lives, hurt families, and create huge health care costs, we share a moral belief that drugs are bad for everyone. To legalize drugs is not to lift high the banner of freedom, but to degrade the standard of morality.

I bring this up because the issue of jealousy is destroying many relationships. If you can only think about those around you in terms of what you can get from them, you don't have love. If you resent putting anyone else's needs first because that is a violation of your rights, you don't have love. Rather than reflecting the love of God, you are reflecting the mind of Satan. A soldier doesn't demand his own way, but obeys the orders of his commander. He has to surrender some of his rights to survive the battle. Likewise, a leader puts the needs of others ahead of himself, so he voluntarily surrenders his rights. In your family, you have to consider the needs of your spouse and your kids ahead of yourself. A loving father isn't jealous of his time, but spends it freely on his kids to help shape their characters for Christ. A loving husband isn't jealous of their money, but allows his wife adequate access for her needs. A loving Christian isn't envious of another's success, but rejoices that the Lord is working in the lives of people.

Jealousy is a natural emotion. From the time I was a baby, I wanted what other people had. I could be playing with my toys and totally ignoring my baseball, but if somebody came in and picked up that ball it instantly became my favorite. At work I didn't just want to do well, I wanted to do better than everybody else. I was born in sin, so I was born with the natural tendency toward jealousy and envy. I could think only of myself. But praise God He changes us. Your natural tendency toward jealousy can be moderated by a supernatural love for others that comes from the Holy Spirit. It really is possible to rejoice with those who rejoice, rather than weeping because someone else has succeeded more than you have. A great leader loves his people and wants them to succeed, even if that means they will outshine him in some area. If you love people, you want them to be successful. Rather than jealously watching over your own rights, ask God for strength to help others succeed.

Love is not boastful or proud.

It took me years to see how my pride was keeping me from enjoying weekends with my wife. We had friends who offered to take our kids for a weekend, but I had said, "No, thanks." I told myself I was too busy to go away for a weekend, that my work was too vitally important to afford time away. Those same friends asked again, but I refused again, and a third time. Finally, my friend asked me, "Is your pride getting in the way of your common sense?" You see, Susy wanted to have that weekend with me! Her house is her office, and she wanted a weekend away from the office. She used to run a section of the legal department at Delta Air Lines; now she runs the washing machine, and she was hoping for a nice break. My pride got in the way. Rather than allowing someone to minister to us, I thought that allowing somebody to take my kids was an admission that I couldn't do it all. I couldn't have a successful legal career, disciple men, raise my children to love God, and foster a healthy marriage all by myself. To allow somebody to take our children, even for a weekend, was to admit my limitations. That's pride.

Our culture has no idea what to do with pride. We're sure that it's a good thing to have, but we hate to see it take over someone's personality. The public schools have spent millions on so-called "self-esteem" programs to boost the pride of students, but so far all that seems to have produced are students who can't read or write and still don't feel good about themselves. The playground is a great place to see pride on display. It used to be that a boy took pride in his play on the field; now he has to display his pride by trash-talking his opponent. The culture of childhood now demands that kids talk about how much they like themselves, yet we've never had a greater need for counselors than we do now.

Pride means having an exaggerated opinion about yourself; to act conceited or haughty or arrogant around others. We used to despise that sort of behavior; now it's fashionable. Television and music stars display their raging arrogance, and *People Magazine* reports it as though it were entertainment. Artists mock those who like their art, then demand money from the Federal coffers to pay for their expressions of angst. Urban professionals dress themselves in the trappings of pride, hoping that the depiction of success will offer them the inner feeling of success. Pride is a national disease, and it has a corrosive effect on families.

To be a successful lawyer, you've got to display some pride. It takes a certain amount of nerve to walk into a courtroom and try to convince a judge and jury that you've done your homework and your arguments are more convincing than your opponent's. I was proud of my success, proud of my firm, and proud of the money I was making. However, consider the impact pride has on one's personality. If everybody is telling you what a great guy you are at the office, then you get home to find your kids have been causing problems, you begin to resent them. "Hey, I'm a big time attorney, and I'm above having to bicker with children about cleaning their rooms." If your wife reminds you that you still haven't completed that handyman project that you've been promising for three months, you think to yourself, "Wait a minute. Today I won a million-dollar lawsuit, and you want to complain about a bathroom drawer that sticks?" Pride builds walls by convincing you that you can live above all these rather mundane problems in life. But life is made up of mundane problems, and if you think your office success will make those disappear, you're fooling yourself.

A proud person says, "I'm better than you. I'm more important that you. You don't count." A humble person says, "You're important. Your voice counts. What do you need?" The great leaders of history have had confidence in themselves, but they saw themselves as tools to be used to assist others in achieving their potential. Christ was a servant first, not a world ruler. George Washington focused his energies on crafting a country, not creating a legend. The two great generals of the Civil War, Robert E. Lee and Ulysses S. Grant, were known for their humility. When Grant first went to Washington, D.C. to meet the President, he wore a private's tunic. No one knew who he was, even though he had recently led the United States Army to its first major victory in more than a year. General Lee once told an aide that his role was to "help guide the men in the right direction, nothing more."

There's nothing wrong with believing in yourself, or in having the confidence that you've done good work. But if you exaggerate your own importance, you'll soon find yourself separated from those around you. Then you're not leading anybody. You've just become your own little one-man parade, announcing to the world what a great person you really are. Without love, you can't be a leader.

CHAPTER SIX

The Loving Leader Part 2

The Christian soldier has to be a leader to his people. One of the qualities of good leadership is that the leader loves his people. Paul continues his message in First Corinthians chapter thirteen with these words:

Love is not rude.

A loving leader takes the time to be polite. Nobody likes to be yelled at. Nobody likes being treated as though he were stupid or insignificant. If you are leading others, you will soon find that people around you make mistakes. People will do the wrong thing. Your spouse will forget something important. Your children will decide something based on ignorance. And you'll be left with the resulting problems and pressures.

When faced with the residue of failure, take extra pains to be polite. I learned a very important truth about projects: People do what makes sense to them. If my kids make a mistake on a gardening project, they usually did what made sense. If a colleague completely dropped one critical part of a project to do something else, it's because he or she thought that was best. People do what make sense to them. That means that they will learn best if you teach them about their mistake and its consequences, rather than to simply start screaming. I've always been impressed with the words of astronaut Jim Lovell, who commanded the Apollo 13 rocket during its disastrous space flight. When praised for remaining calm and polite during the life-threatening crisis, he said that he had simply done what made sense. "We could have yelled and pointed fingers at each other, but in the end we would still be stuck in a dead spacecraft, thousands of miles from earth." So he kept control of his crew by remaining calm and treating everyone with respect. "My goal was to always try and treat the others the way I would have wanted to be treated," he said.

The loving leader isn't rude. He uses words to encourage and instruct people rather than attack. He treats people with respect, rather than lording his position over them. Solomon says that "a man of wisdom uses words with restraint." We're all going to face tough times, but the mature man of God will remain polite in the face of trials. "Consider it all joy, my brethren," James says, "when you encounter various trials, knowing that the testing of your faith produces endurance" (James 1:2-3).

The Bible is full of instruction for how Christians should use their mouths, because God knows that the mouth causes no end of trouble for people. That's why James adds the thought, "Let everyone be quick to hear, slow to speak and slow to anger; for the anger of man does not achieve the righteousness of God" (vv. 19-20). But if you have a heart for people, you'll see your words as a chance to encourage rather than to criticize, to bolster rather than to break.

This has been a really tough lesson for me to learn. In a courtroom, you use your words to attack the other side. So when I took that lesson home I would sometimes continue to attack with my words, deeply wounding my wife. But when I came to Christ, I realized I had to begin using my words to build up, not just to tear down. As I began to pray for the Lord to give me a heart for people, I began seeing an opportunity to use words constructively rather than destructively. Paul says in Ephesians 4:29, "Do not let any unwholesome talk come out of your mouths, but only what is helpful for building others up according to their needs, that it may benefit those who listen."

Rather than pointing out what my children had done wrong, I began looking for ways to verbally express what they had done right. Rather than trying to solve my wife's problems, I began to repeat the problem back to her, to let her know I understood it. By speaking that way, I personalized the issue and showed that I could identify with it. Then I'd say something like, "That must hurt." By expressing my understanding of her pain, I was politely allowing her to reveal herself. A rule for communicating that I've used for several years is this: Respond to emotion with emotion, respond to fact with fact. Susy used to offer me some emotion ("I was late because the car won't start!"), and I'd respond with fact ("If you press the accelerator all the way to the floor, you won't have any trouble."). But she didn't want fact. When she gave me emotion, she wanted me to connect to her emotionally ("That's too bad. I hate it when that happens."). Then when she comes at me with fact ("I need you to take the car to the mechanic"), I can respond with fact ("I'll take it in tomorrow").

Not long after I arrived at CBMC, I sat through a lengthy strategic planning session, at which we hoped to evaluate where the ministry was and decide how to best achieve the mission of the organization. The key to strategic planning is to become aware of the critical event for your ministry, and for years our conclusion had been that we needed to get men to pray to receive Christ. Everything we did was focused on that event. However in this meeting it seemed that God was not drawing us toward that conclusion, and I became frustrated and irritated because we didn't seem to be making any progress. Every time I tried to move us forward I hit another roadblock; I simply had to keep my mouth shut in love, not respond rudely, and allow God to work through the people in that room to reach a breakthrough. Eventually we came to the conclusion that there was not a critical event, but rather a critical process whereby a person moves from not believing in Christ to believing, and eventually toward maturity in Christ. That process has now become the grid by which all our activity at CBMC is measured. By waiting on the Lord and not responding in impatience and rudeness, I was able to see God dump in our laps the key to our strategic plan.

Polite and impolite words can significantly alter your relationship. Imagine the last time you were treated rudely by someone on the phone. It changes your entire outlook on your day. We were at a restaurant recently, and I was going along fine until we encountered a waitress with an attitude. Suddenly the whole meal was shot. I was unhappy with the food, in a sour mood, and ready to leave. On the other hand, a few encouraging words from Susy can smooth over that troubled water and set everything right again. A loving leader has a heart for people, and uses his words to build them up.

Love is not selfish.

Why do most divorces occur? It isn't over sex, money, in-laws, or communication. Those are only the manifestations of the real problem. I'll bet ninety-nine percent of marriages that break up do so because of selfishness. I want my way. I want it all the time. I'm willing to give up a little ground, but only if I think doing so will give me an advantage at another time, so that I can get my way again. A leader too much concerned with his own welfare can never enjoy the confidence of those around him. They won't trust him, and they'll soon begin developing their own little kingdoms so that they can be selfish, too.

After becoming a Christian, it was natural that I wanted to share my tremendous joy with my friends and business colleagues. However, I came on too strong, said too much, and appeared very judgmental in trying to encourage others to see the merits of Christ. Frankly, my approach was not always very loving, although my bottom line was, "I love these people so much I'll take the risk to share my faith in hopes of saving them from damnation." But I found that my good motives were misunderstood, until I began to communicate on the basis that I cared personally for the individuals and wanted to help them with their felt needs. My help for them wasn't contingent upon any response of theirs, nor upon their interest in spiritual things.

For example, when Jason came to our firm, he was like the others we'd hired—the best of the best. We had sifted through hundreds of applicants from all the top schools in the country and had selected Jason to join us. He was there just a short time when I went into his office one day and casually mentioned I was glad he was there. He was brand new, and I was viewed as one of the guys in charge, so he was pretty nervous about me sitting in his office without a clear legal agenda. Then I mentioned that he was one of the best new-hires we'd ever had, and that I was convinced he could reach every degree of success in the firm that I had if he simply followed three or four principles that would help him realize his dreams. I offered to discuss those principles with him at some point in the future, thanked him for his time, and returned to my office. I had barely sat down when I heard a knock on my door and saw Jason, wondering if I would like to go for lunch! People always have time for others who are sincerely interested in their problems.

We are all basically selfish. We all want things for ourselves, and want things our own way. The biggest struggle you'll have in marriage is the discovery that life will never again be the way it was when you were single. Many newly married people are totally shocked to find that they are selfish; they never considered it before, since they had no one to compare themselves to. Once you get married, you find that two people will not always agree on issues, and someone will not get his or her way. Sometimes that means one person becomes completely dominant, demanding his or her own way at all times. This individual is an emotional baby, crying when he doesn't get what he wants. Those sorts of relationships rarely last, for no one wants to be subservient forever. So the battle most of us face is this: How can we not be selfish? How does one learn to be selfless?

A loving leader is devoted to the success of those around him. Again, consider the example of Jesus Christ. He took pains to look out for the interests of others over His own. He served others sacrificially. He helped the disciples grow in their faith and knowledge of God. On the cross, He arranged for someone to care for His mother. Paul, in speaking of the example Jesus set for us, says, "Do nothing out of selfish ambition or vain conceit, but in humility consider others better than yourselves. Each of you should look not only to your own interests, but also to the interests of others" (Philippians 2:3-4). Imagine following a leader who treated others better than he treats himself. That's the example of Jesus Christ. Who would you rather follow into battle: Someone who is primarily concerned with his own interests, or one who is more concerned with the interests of others? As a soldier, I want my leader to be thinking about me when the bullets start flying! I want him to be taking the best interests of his soldiers to heart.

Paul goes on to tell us,

"Your attitude should be the same as that of Christ Jesus:
Who, being in very nature God,
    did not consider equality with God
    something to be grasped,
But made Himself nothing,
    taking the very nature of a servant,
    being made in human likeness,
    and being found in appearance as a man,
He humbled Himself
    and became obedient to death—
    even death on a cross!
Therefore God exalted Him to the highest place
And gave Him the name that is above every name,
That at the Name of Jesus every knee should bow,
    in heaven and on earth and under the earth,
And every tongue confess that Jesus Christ is Lord,
    to the glory of God the Father."

(Philippians 2:5-11)

Those are some of my favorite verses in all of Scripture. Jesus Christ is God. He had full authority and power as God, but He chose to make Himself nothing and become a man. He chose to make Himself a servant. He chose to obey the Father and die, even though as a man he did not want to die. And it is because of His obedience that the Father has exalted Him. Love isn't selfish, it's unselfish. It is sacrificial, actively working on behalf of others. That's the example Christ set for us. That's the perfect description of the loving leader.

Love is not easily angered.

When you pray for a heart for people, you'll find the Lord suddenly gives you plenty of opportunity to love others. When I prayed that God would give me a heart for others, I was immediately inundated with needs. I saw men who were suffering in their jobs. I met women who were in the midst of terrible emotional pain in their marriages. I began meeting more and more unsaved people who were on the path to an eternity apart from Jesus Christ. And I began to love them. I started seeing them not as people with problems, but as people with possibilities for God. Instead of ignoring their pain, I began to connect with their pain, and in doing so I connected with the individuals. I began to see the hurt others were experiencing, and how Christ could help. And that made me considerably more patient.

I'll see men in their offices snap at a secretary or yell at an underling, and it makes me think of myself fifteen years ago. I would do the same things, because I was a selfish person. I wanted things done my way, on my time schedule, according to my goals. If anything got in the way of that agenda, I'd be easily angered. Sometimes I would yell, other times I'd throw things. It was my way of working off steam, I told myself. But, actually, it was my own selfishness at work.

I wish I could say that this problem has been completely conquered in my life; however, just as an alcoholic has to take life one day at a time with his temptation for drink, I too must take it one day at a time with my temptation for self-centeredness, expressed in anger. Even as a mature Christian, I'm embarrassed to confess that from time to time I'm just not very pleasant to be around. This is usually a function of my trust quotient; that is, the extent to which my problems are God's versus the extent to which I seek to control them.

A number of years ago, an example of that occurred when my good friend Sally filled in at the office, handling my calls during a very busy time for the ministry. She followed instructions perfectly, but because I was on the phone, I missed a very important call that I'd been waiting for. Because I was in charge that day, rather than the Lord, I took it upon myself to remedy the problem before praying about it or giving God time to work in my heart. I simply marched up to Sally's desk and, standing above her, offered a three-point lecture on how she could have handled the situation better, ignoring the fact that she had handled it exactly as she'd been told. I justified my own conduct by telling myself that I had missed a very important call, and I wasn't jumping up and down or screaming, but my tone and demeanor were everything but loving and gentle. Sally went home in tears, and I in frustration. That evening I had to call and apologize to her, and she graciously forgave me in what I thought would be the end of a very bad day. But the next morning, as I arrived at my office, Fred, the man who is my right arm on the ministry leadership team, confronted me over my ungodly conduct the previous day. I'd like to tell you that I received his comments with grace and humility, but that's not the case. It was clear I had not dealt with the problem as deeply as I should, as my defensiveness revealed. My justification was that I'd had a bad day, missed an important call, and Sally had forgiven me, but Fred wasn't content to let it lie there. Much to my chagrin, he asked the other members of the leadership team to join him in confronting me with this weakness. This was particularly humiliating, since I'd been all over the country testifying as to my new life in Christ, which had delivered me from a temper that was known for punching walls and throwing verbal tirades. The Lord was seeking to show me through Fred that, while progress had been made, more was needed.

It took a lot for Fred to take the risk to confront his "boss" in such a personal way, but that's how much Fred loves me. He's willing to step out, as a leader committed to Christ, and speak to a friend who needed help with a blind spot. I'm thankful to be surrounded by men like Fred, who is an accountability partner for me, especially on the subjects of my temper and how I respond to others during a time of stress.

A mature, unselfish soldier wants people to do well, but he isn't easily angered when things don't go his way. Instead, he patiently helps develop people so that they can get it right the next time. Jesus didn't scream at Peter for denying him; instead the Lord patiently talked with Peter to help him understand the importance of fulfilling his role. Peter was feeling bad enough about denying Christ three times; scolding him wouldn't have done much good. So the Lord forgave Peter and told him he had a job to do: "Feed my sheep." Peter was never the same. The guy who, days earlier, had called down curses on his own head, insisting he didn't know Jesus, was now declaring the truth of the gospel in the temple courts. The man who had cowered at the sight of the temple guard was now rejoicing that he was counted worthy to suffer disgrace for the name of Jesus. Peter changed because Jesus was not easily angered. Christ showed Peter how much He loved him.

If you are going to enter the battle as a soldier, pray for the Lord to give you a heart for people. Ask Him to open your eyes so that you can see their needs, feel their pain, and help them. God can do great things with a few men who really love others. When Robert Murray McShane was a young man, he recognized the need the people of Scotland had for the good news of Jesus Christ. He spent long hours in prayer over the matter, eventually echoing the prayer of Hannah by saying, "Give me Scotland or I die!" His love compelled him to cry out to God for the souls of other people. Who are you crying out for? Who do you have a heart for?

Love keeps no record of wrongs.

Science tells us that two things can't occupy the same space at the same time. Love and bitterness cannot occupy the same heart. If you really love someone, you will let go of the past. That's a hard message for many people, particularly Christian women who have been married to hard men. A guy who has been angry for years can suddenly come to Christ and be full of love, but his wife still has the years of pain to deal with. She might be bitter, so she will have to pray for a new love. She'll have to act in her husband's best interests, even though she may not feel like it. She will have to express love to him, even though there may not be any feeling of love inside her. It's a tough job, but it's what Christians are called to do.

That's what Susy did. She prayed that God would give her a new love for me, because my uncaring behavior had destroyed her love. My hardness and negative attitudes had put out the flame of love my wife had for me. But as a Christian, she knew God wanted her to love me. Praise the Lord for answering her prayer. Over time, Susy was able to rebuild her love for this sorry husband.

Christians can't keep a record of wrongs. All the hard words, all the critical comments need to be put behind you. You can't do it on your own; it will require the power of God to forgive, but forgive you must. If you cannot put away that record of wrongs that you have against others, you'll never experience the freedom and joy Christ intends for you to have.

When Jesus told the parable of the unmerciful servant in Matthew chapter eighteen, His point was not just that we have been forgiven much. The Lord notes at the end of that story, "This is how my heavenly Father will treat each of you unless you forgive your brother from your heart" (Matthew 18:35). God loves you and wants to be in a right relationship with you, but He cannot be if you are storing up a record of wrongs done to you by others. Forgiveness can free you.

I know a woman who was so bitter she was described as hard by her friends. She had good reason to be bitter—her husband was a jerk of the first order, who had hurt her badly before falling into a deep depression and attempting suicide. That gal needed to experience forgiveness, but she never could until she forgave her husband. When I saw her not long ago, I didn't recognize her. Her face was different, her entire countenance changed. I knew immediately what had happened. She had forgiven her husband for the list of wrongs committed, and in doing so she changed her life. Her outlook, her attitudes, and her ability to serve others were all radically different because she could now experience forgiveness.

Of all the teachers I've had in my life, the ones I have appreciated the most are those who have not dealt with past mistakes, but who look at future possibilities. Rather than criticizing me, they've moved ahead with a positive attitude, convinced they could help this poor jarhead learn. If I spent all my time focused on my mistakes, I'd never get anything done. So instead of focusing on the slip-ups, I try to confess my mistakes, right the wrong, and focus on new areas for growing.

One thing I've learned about Christ is that He didn't keep a record of wrongs. He forgave Peter for denying Him. He forgave those who condemned Him, and while hanging on the cross asked His Father to forgive those who put Him to death. He is calling us to love others in that same way.

Love rejoices in the truth.

Love doesn't delight in evil. A loving leader takes no pleasure in someone's failure. He wants everyone to experience the surpassing joy that comes in knowing Jesus Christ. Men, it is your responsibility to make sure your wife and children love the Lord. That's a message that gets watered down in our culture, but it's very plain in Scripture. You are to love your wife the way Christ loved the church. If you reflect the pure love of

God to your wife, she won't be able to resist it. People are longing for God, anxious for an encounter with the Almighty. So if you present it to her, she'll embrace it. Let the Lord love your wife through you. Care for her, sacrificially love her, and protect her. God has entrusted her to your care. Let her see Jesus Christ in you.

Soldiers in the battlefield need an example to follow, so they often select the best soldiers to be the standard-bearers for the unit. When new guys come along, they just have to look to the standard-bearer to see what a good soldier is like. Let your wife and kids see what a mature man of God is like by manifesting your faith through your life. Children growing up are told that God is their Heavenly Father, and they'll relate that fact to their earthly fathers. If a father is distant and harsh, the child will see God as being distant and harsh. If the father is gentle and loving, he'll see what the true God is really like. You rejoice in the truth when you reflect the life of God in you to your spouse and your kids.

Love protects, trusts, hopes, and perseveres.

All four of these words describe love as an action that flows from a positive attitude. A person who loves others is a positive person, and that is reflected in his or her behavior. For example, we're told that love always protects. If your wife knows that you'll protect her from the flak that is sure to come your way, she'll love you. Sometimes someone will hurt me, and since Susy and I share hurt, I'll tell her about the pain. But there are always two sides to events, and I try to share the other person's point of view to keep her from becoming angry with the other person while she helps me gain perspective on my pain. By keeping a positive attitude about my work and its impact on others, I'm revealing my love for my wife.

Another thing that we're told is that love always trusts. That means my wife keeps a positive attitude toward me, even during difficult times. For example, I have to travel quite a bit each year, representing CBMC at meetings around the country. Each time I walk into a new hotel room, I call my wife and we pray together. She trusts that I'll be faithful to her, and I've never given her reason not to trust me. Her positive response to me is a reflection of her love for me. If your wife knows she can trust you, even when you're going away on a business trip, she'll love you.

Looked at another way, Susy knows that she can trust what I'll say about our relationship. I've seen wives of speakers sit nervously, twisting their napkins, wondering what secrets the husbands might reveal. I can help my wife keep a positive attitude by giving her reason to trust me on this issue. I always check to make sure any examples I use are acceptable to her, so that there are no surprises when she hears me speak. By doing so, I'm showing her that I love her and care about her feelings.

Paul also says that love always hopes. If your family hears you talking about your hope in Christ, they'll love you. The strength that comes to a family led by a godly man is incredible. The dad who proves he is strong enough to make a public stand for Christ shows how much he loves his wife and kids. He wants them to know that he isn't ashamed of the Lord, and that he prays for their own spiritual growth. He takes a positive approach to the faith which rubs off on his family. "These words, which I am commanding you today, shall be on your heart; and you shall teach them diligently to your sons and shall talk of them when you sit in your house and when you walk by the way and when you lie down and when you rise up" (Deuteronomy 6:6-7).

Men, be the spiritual leader in your home. Pray with your wife. Let your kids see you reading your Bible. Talk naturally about spiritual things. Take everybody to church on Sunday mornings with a positive attitude, and say encouraging things to your family about the pastor and the worship service. Your family will feed off your hope.

Your family should see the results of your quiet time in your life. A joke around our house is that whenever I say to my kids, "Hey, I think I'll skip my quiet time today so that we can get some things done around the house," they'll respond, "No thanks, Dad! You do your quiet time. We'll keep busy until you're finished." My children know that their dad without a quiet time is too much of me and not enough of Jesus. But with a quiet time, the odds increase that the family will have a more spiritual, relaxed, and focused father, ready to take on the day's activities with them as a great adventure and service to the Lord. We've got to let our children see the power of Christ through our successes and our failures, with the appropriate confessions and requests for forgiveness when warranted.

During my Operation Timothy Bible study with my daughter Anna, I told her how sorry I was that I had gotten mad at her mother. "Oh, that's okay, Daddy," she said to me. "I liked seeing how to resolve arguments." It's one thing to encourage our kids to read the Bible and memorize Scripture, but it's another to let them quiz us on the verses we're memorizing. The former approach suggests hypocrisy—"Do as I say, not as I do." The latter approach teaches them the importance of diligence, and offers a first-hand view of the results of memorizing! If God is conforming your mind to His thinking, it should be evident to your children. If you're generally negative toward Bible reading or your church, your kids will be, too, so show them how positive you are about your faith.

Finally, Paul says that love perseveres. None of this is easy. It will grow over time, and it will require you to have a positive attitude and be willing to sacrifice your desires for the needs of someone else. But if you will persevere you'll see real changes occur in your marriage and family. Love changes lives. Leaders are to persevere in love and watch the lives of those around them be changed by it.

Love is mature.

The last few verses of First Corinthians chapter thirteen have to do with putting away the childish things and moving on to maturity. That's what the loving leader does. He recognizes that he is in a battle, and that battles are not won by individuals, but by armies. So to help craft a strong army, he loves his people. It takes great maturity to be selfless. Only a mature individual can put the needs of another over his own needs. It takes a mature man to be polite, to use encouraging words, and to keep a positive attitude in the face of strong opposition.

But a mature man of God is marked by his love. He loves God, and it shows through his strong spiritual life. He also loves people, which he reveals through his selfless actions on their behalf. Too many Christians think that leadership means getting the perks and running the show, when it actually means facing the toughest tests and serving others. Pray for God to make you unselfish. Pray for Him to give you a heart for people. You'll find that a life filled with love will make you a better soldier and a more capable leader.

CHAPTER SEVEN

Self-Controlled Soldiers

L ike a city whose walls are broken down is a man who lacks self-control" (Proverbs 25:28). Judging by our culture today, the walls are broken down everywhere. We live in an age of instant gratification. We have instant breakfast, fast food lunches, and meal-in-a-minute microwave dinners. We have instant access on the computer, we don't wait in lines at banks if we can use the ATM, and our automobiles have been turned over to places that can do an oil change in ten minutes and a tune-up in thirty. Even the things that used to take a long time have become instant. We expect our dry cleaning to be done in a half-hour, our film to be developed while we wait, and our glasses to be sized and ground in no more than sixty minutes. We rush everywhere for everything, so that our lives have turned into one long sprint. We especially don't want to wait for anything, so we've developed credit cards that advertise with slogans like, "Why wait? Buy that car now!" In a world of instant gratification, how in the world does a soldier develop self-control?

A person who has self-control is able to restrain or give direction to his desires, actions, and emotions. He understands the power of delayed gratification. Rather than being ruled by his passions, he is ruled by his principles. He carefully chooses what he will do. It requires personal discipline to live that way, and that is an excellent place for a Christian soldier to begin. When we were basically an agrarian society, we lived by seasons and understood the importance of sowing and reaping. Our instant society has lost the concept of waiting for the harvest. We expect the payoff immediately. We want people to change right away when they hear the truth, even though that's not how most people work. The apostle Paul spoke of having one man sow, another man water, and a third man reap. He understood that some things take time. The Scottish people have a saying: "It takes nine months to have a baby— you can't put nine women on it and get it done in a month!"

If you are going to lead others into battle, you can't jump at the first opportunity that presents itself. You've got to consider your actions carefully. You've got to think through your overall plan. A commander weighs his options, then decides based on principle rather than passion. He may be angry, and desire to send his troops storming into the jungle to wipe out the enemy. But if he doesn't know where the enemy is, or he allows his passions to blind him to the danger, he could be sending his men to die needlessly. Instead, he bases his decision whether to fight on principles.

A problem we have in our modern era is that most men aren't sure what their principles are, so the first step to gaining self-control is to determine your limitations. Where are you weak? What leads you into sin? Where are your walls broken down?

In 1 John 2:15-18, we are warned, "Do not love the world or anything in the world. If anyone loves the world, the love of the Father is not in him." Right away the apostle warns against embracing the things of this world, then he goes on to describe them: "For everything in the world—the cravings of sinful man, the lust of his eyes, and the boasting of what he has and does—comes not from the Father but from the world. The world and its desires pass away, but the man who does the will of God lives forever." In that passage John names the three areas of temptation that make war on our self-control. First there is the "cravings of sinful man," which refers to sensual pleasure. Second is the "lust of the eyes," a reference to coveting wealth and opulence. Third is the "boasting of what he has and does," which is simply pride. Each of those areas pose a tremendous challenge to the man who wants to be a spiritual soldier.

The Cravings of Sinful Man

Our culture inundates us with messages about sensual pleasure. Television commercials portray cars not as dependable, long-lasting vehicles, but as sexy, comfortable machines. Shampoo ads don't suggest that they'll clean your hair, but that they'll draw women to your side. Commercials for clothes aren't based on the material's quality or wear, but on their sexiness and look. Everything from beer to tires are sold with sex appeal, so that the consumer will equate sensuality with the advertised product. With that sort of constant input, it's no wonder we're struggling with cravings.

One of the issues that trips men up is that of food. A man with no self-control can never say "no" to an extra helping, or "yes" to an exercise program. Yet when a guy is fifty pounds overweight, he loses his ability to talk to a nonbeliever about "surrendering to God" or "allowing the Lord to take control." An overweight man displays his lack of self-control, and it allows others to question his heart. I know, because I was there. I used to have what a friend calls "furniture disease"— my chest kept falling into my drawers!

I remember speaking at a luncheon when I was in need of dropping thirty pounds. I couldn't run a mile or do more than twenty push-ups. The Spirit pricked my conscience with a question: What do people think when they see a fat guy talk about self-control?

So I made up my mind to lose the weight. It was a decision I hated. I like to eat, and the thought of saying no to good food is awful. Worse, I hate to run. I decided to run for thirty minutes most days, and some days I hate every minute of it. Years ago I began getting up very early each morning so that I could spend time with the Lord. I hate getting up early. Now I have to get up even earlier so that I can also run. I hate it! I hate turning off my alarm clock while it's still dark and getting out from under the warm covers onto a cold floor. But I do it every morning because it puts down the flesh. I don't want my body to control me. I don't want to be a slave to my appetites. I want to live on principle, controlling my body. Paul says, "Do you not know that in a race all the runners run, but only one gets the prize? Run in such a way as to get the prize. Everyone who competes in the games goes into strict training. They do it to get a prize that will not last; but we do it to get a prize that will last forever. Therefore I do not run like a man running aimlessly; I do not fight like a man beating the air. No, I beat my body and make it my slave so that after I have preached to others, I myself will not be disqualified for the prize" (1 Corinthians 9:24-27). Can you claim those verses for your own life? How many men do you know who make their body a slave so as to more effectively preach the good news of Jesus Christ? When Hudson Taylor knew the Lord was calling him into Christian service, he began the practice of denying himself luxuries, to best prepare himself for the mission field. Men who are going into battle have to develop self-control. They have to be willing to go without and to suffer if they expect to win, for victory will belong to those who are well-prepared and well-trained. One thing I learned in Viet Nam is that lazy soldiers get themselves and others killed. The sluggish and careless get blown up or shot. The cautious survive.

If you're going to be a soldier, get control of your body. Think about what you're eating. Keep your body in shape. Get up early and spend time with the Lord each day, so that you begin your day thinking the thoughts of the Lord. If you need to, find a partner to hold you accountable to your plan. Call each other in the morning to make sure you're both up, and pray for each other over the phone before going to the Word. Whatever it takes, make the decision to establish control over your body, rather than being a slave to the flesh.

The other major area of fleshly craving is lust. Many Christian marriages are hurting because the man is struggling with thoughts of impurity. There is an abundance of temptation that attacks men all day long. Sex is in advertisements, in magazines, in music, in movies, on television, on radio—it's almost impossible to go through life these days and not have sex thrust at you. Most men are visually stimulated, so a Christian man walking through a maze of female flesh is like taking a kid through a candy factory but telling him he can't touch anything. He is regularly reminded of the importance of sex, but the Lord makes clear he is only to experience sex within the confines of his marriage. Any loss of self-control can be devastating. There's a war going on, and Satan is determined to destroy Christian men by throwing sensual temptation at men with poor self-control.

A friend of mine owned a huge corporation and began a successful ministry on the side. But Talbert really struggled with sexual temptation. He was a good guy, a man's man who knew everything the Scriptures had to say about purity, but he couldn't control his own body. He got involved in pornography, and his wife eventually left him. It ruined his credibility. They tried getting together again, this time at a couple's retreat sponsored by his company, but she caught him early one morning trying to sneak a peek in a women's bedroom. Their marriage ended, and so did his ministry. His lack of self-control got him disqualified from ministry. His company is still profitable, but his life isn't.

The amazing thing is that we all know men who have experienced that. Pornography, prostitution, and affairs seem to be the order of the day. Where are the righteous men who will take a stand for purity? I recently counseled a man who was having an affair. He knew it was wrong, and that it would only lead to trouble. He agreed with me as we looked through the Bible to find all the passages that spoke of purity and personal holiness. But in the end his message to me was, "I just can't give her up." He lost his wife, his family, his good name, and eventually his business because he couldn't exercise self-control.

I once counseled a man who was an elected official of his state, after having retired from law practice. He was having an affair, and I gave him both barrels from the Bible. I preached purity at that guy, but he couldn't seem to get control over his own body. Every time he swore he would never see her again, he'd drive by her house, start thinking about their escapades, and the next thing he knew he was ringing her doorbell. He was a slave to his passions. That man has now been accused of helping his girlfriend in a plot to kill his wife.

Men aren't the only ones involved in this battle. I've been to plenty of Christian retreats where I saw women reading romance novels that were full of explicit sexual scenes. They're nothing less than pornography with a pretty cover. One Christian woman I know, whose husband was neglecting her, tried a number of places to find someone with whom she could be close. She finally started spending her time on the Internet, and met a man who was sensitive, responsive, and attentive to her. She gave her emotion to him, and wound up filing for divorce. The good news is that her husband changed his behavior and won her back, but that's the exception rather than the rule. The divorce rate inside the church is nearly the same as the divorce rate outside the church, so our churches apparently are not full of men and women practicing self-control.

Picture a guy who has spent his day driving into town looking at the billboards and listening to the radio. He hears a few rough comments from the men he works with, and he can't help but notice the advertisements in the magazines lying in the lobby of his business. After going past those same billboards at night, once again hearing the songs and ads on the radio, that man walks in the door at home, struggling with having been bombarded with sexual images, and he needs to experience openness and gentleness from his wife. He needs someone who will understand his needs and love him. After all that temptation, he needs to spend time with the one he loves. He needs to gain control of his mind and body, and experience the joy of embracing his lifelong love in the sanctity of his own home. If he doesn't find affection at home, his mind starts to think back over all those images he has seen. He's been experiencing images of sensual pleasure, but he has promised himself to be true to his wife. He wants to keep his mind true to his bride, but if he comes home and gets no affection, it's like taking that kid through the candy store, then handing him nothing but burnt toast.

A doctor friend, who has led many men to Christ, is in crisis. He is an expert at repairing broken bones, but he can't repair the brokenness caused by one embrace and a few kisses with the wrong woman. His married life had grown sort of stale, and he found himself attracted to a female patient. One day he did something he thought he would never do. He leaned over and kissed her. It was a stupid mistake. He didn't fall into bed with her, he just gave her one kiss, but that one lapse of self-control ruined his life. The woman talked with the medical authorities, and several others made complaints. He lost his medical partnership, and his license is now in jeopardy. He fell into disgrace in his community. Worse than that, he had to tell his unsaved daughter why he is no longer the faithful Christian husband and respected physician he used to be. Like a city without walls, his lack of self-control left him unprotected and allowed his career to be destroyed. When I talked with that man's wife recently about her husband's sin, she said to me, "Phil, it's my fault too. I didn't offer him anything but burnt toast."

Husbands and wives have a responsibility to one another. They are to give themselves to one another, lovingly and completely. "The husband should fulfill his marital duty to his wife, and likewise the wife to her husband. The wife's body does not belong to her alone but also to her husband. In the same way, the husband's body does not belong to him alone but also to his wife" (1 Corinthians 7:3-4). Wife, you can minister to your husband and help him remain true to you by showing him affection and understanding. Husband, you can minister to your wife and help her remain satisfied and loved by showing her attention and protection. Talk with her. Listen to her. Show a little romance. Tell her about your struggle to remain true to her only. That will help build a wall around your integrity, and keep you protected from the attacks of Satan.

The Lust of the Eyes

I think more Christian men struggle with money than they do with extra-marital affairs. Nobody wants to talk about it, since the desire for wealth is part of American culture. But 1

John says that God's people are not to be part of this world's system. Christians have bought into the culture, even though it is in direct opposition to God's Word, and they spend their time thinking about money rather than thinking about the Lord. "Do not store up for yourselves treasures on earth, where moth and rust destroy, and where thieves break in and steal," Jesus said. "But store up for yourselves treasures in heaven, where moth and rust do not destroy, and where thieves do not break in and steal. For where your treasure is, there your heart will be also" (Matthew 6:19-21).

The trappings of success won't last very long, yet most of us are much more concerned with our earthly wealth than our heavenly abundance. We spend a lot more time worrying about indebtedness than worrying about our neighbor's salvation. We believe we've got to keep up with the Joneses. Think about it: How many of the things you've bought in the last year were absolute necessities to life? Look through your checkbook and you'll find the things that are most important to you. I've talked with couples who made it sound like big houses, new cars, and expensive toys were essentials to modern living. That's wrong, and it's nothing but a lie from Satan to keep you enslaved in his worldly system.

I don't think you need to drive a beat-up old Rambler or live in a trailer to be spiritual, but consider what values your attitude toward money reveals. If you spent thousands on golf but little on God, you value recreation more than you value your relationship to the Lord. If you spent a fortune on travel but little on tithes, you value your own good times more than you value the gospel. Remember, a soldier isn't overly concerned with the trappings of his camp; he just wants to win the battle. If you are more concerned with money than you are with God, you're in trouble. "No one can serve two masters," the Lord said in Matthew 6:24. "Either he will hate the one and love the other, or he will be devoted to the one and despise the other. You cannot serve both God and money." So, who are you serving?

It's easy to lose our perspective when talking about money, since we have so much of it. We are rich in earthly goods, but poor in heavenly assets. Christ once warned that it is easier for a camel to go through the eye of a needle than for a rich man to enter the kingdom of God. Who would you say is rich? Is it the top five percent of the population? Then you probably qualify, since the average working American is in the top five percent of wage earners in the world. In other words, it's easier to get a camel through the eye of a needle than for you to get into heaven. Those are strong words, so you'd better make sure your wealth represents your relationship with God.

I've met quite a few men who have become captive to the cost structure. They want to give more to Christian ministries, but they can never afford it. Some of them want to quit their jobs and work for a ministry, but they can't see how God would take care of them. They feel trapped in their jobs, but the trap is one of their own making. "Who of you by worrying can add a single hour to his life?…Do not worry, saying, 'What shall we eat?' or 'What shall we drink?' or 'What shall we wear?' For the pagans run after all these things, and your Heavenly Father knows that you need them. But seek first His kingdom and His righteousness, and all these things will be given to you as well" (Matthew 6:27, 31-34).

If you and your wife are struggling with your budget, find a godly couple to whom the Lord has entrusted great resources, and ask them to share their struggles. One couple close to us has tremendous wealth, but are uncommonly comfortable with who they are, generous with their resources, and humble in their conviction that they "did nothing to deserve the money." They see themselves as stewards of those resources on behalf of God. That couple has had a great impact on our children, sharing their deep sense of responsibility for using and investing those resources wisely. They are neither embarrassed nor prideful about their wealth, but simply look upon money as an important responsibility given them by the Lord.

Another family has accumulated wealth for over five generations through a family owned, Christ-centered business. I've had the pleasure of knowing four generations of this family, and they have all been marked by several qualities. First, they see their wealth as a gift from the Lord. Second, they are passionate about giving to causes that will lead others to the saving knowledge of Jesus Christ. Third, they are active in personal giving to an extent that would shock most people. They intentionally find ways to endure sacrifice to avoid the "spoiling" that resources can bring. Fourth, they all have a tremendous work ethic, requiring excellence in their own lives.

If you keep buying things to make yourself feel better, you're caught in Satan's trap. Things like that never last. Cars wear out. Clothes go out of style. Toys break. If you're working sixty hours a week to support your wife's buying habits, you're a slave to money. All that time at the mall is just another of Satan's tricks to keep you in slavery. If he can keep you chasing after opulence, he knows you've been removed from the battle.

I know a man who had a great head for business. He worked as an adviser for a Christian money management ministry, and he really knew his stuff. He helped people invest their income, and he produced more money than anybody I've ever met. But he spent it faster than he could make it. He had no self-control. Rather than living on a budget, he was living out of his pocket. There was no wall, no protection around him, and Satan used it to destroy his life. His spending habits drove him from ministry, forced him into bankruptcy, and took him out of the battle.

It's easy for a Christian to get caught up in spending money, especially when he begins earning more of it. I was once speaking at a conference, and on my way back I had some time to kill at the airport so I wandered into one of the little handicraft shops. They were selling things made of jade, and they were really beautiful. I bought a couple figurines as gifts, then they made m : such a good deal that I added some bracelets for my gi' .s, and some gifts for other family members. There was also a centerpiece which I knew would be beautiful, and they gave me such a great price I had to have it. I hate to admit it, but I ended up spending a ton of money on things that I didn't need. It was as if I had no self-control. When I got home I happily showed it to Susy, who exercised her own self-control by not throttling me on the spot. She really handled it well, appreciated the pieces, but politely suggested we didn't have the money to spend on jade gifts. Susy was right, of course, so I agreed to send it all back. (But I didn't...I chickened out and Susy sent it all back!) I was like a city whose walls are broken down—no self-control, thus no protection. I've found that when I don't have a budget to live by, or don't exercise the self-control to live by it, we seem to have financial troubles. I learned early in my Christian life to tithe and give the Lord His portion of my salary, or that the alternative was financial troubles. If I fail to exercise self-control over my purchases, we can expect financial challenges. No salary is high enough for a man without self-control.

I'll never forget one of the worst days of my life, when I sat in the offices of Ron Blue, founder of a financial and estate planning firm headquartered in Atlanta, listening to former professional football player Monty Johnson describe our situation. Susy and I both were working, and we had a good income, but our problem was that our spending exceeded our income. The difference was debt, and Monty showed us through his blackboard illustrations that our spending was out of control. My mind flashed back to those days in law school, when I used to hear about smart lawyers helping dumb football players manage their finances so that they wouldn't go broke. So here we were, two lawyers so dumb we had to be told by a football player how to better manage our funds! Susy and I will be forever grateful for the teachings of Ron Blue and Larry Burkett, who helped us get our finances under control so that we could eventually go into full-time ministry.

A soldier can't be double-minded. He can't have his mind filled with worries about money, or he won't be properly prepared for the battle. A soldier who is going to be leading others needs to focus on the battle. "No one serving as a soldier gets involved with civilian affairs," Paul tells Timothy in 2 Timothy 2:4. If you expect to lead others into Christian warfare, you've got to set an example for them by having self-control over your spending habits. Create a realistic budget. A budget is nothing more than plan for your money. It might be a hard or a soft budget, but create something so that you are in control of where your money is going, rather than having your money simply disappear on temporal things.

If your salary just won't stretch far enough, you've only got two choices: Bring in more money or cut expenses. Since most of us cannot automatically bring in more money, make the hard choices to cut expenses. It may mean making a sacrifice, but the freedom you'll feel will make up for it. Learn to live on a budget, and make sure to make tithing part of it. God demands the first portion of your income, and it's been my experience that if I fail to give it to Him, it will disappear through extra costs or useless purchases. Without those three things—a budget, tithing, and self-control—you'll never have financial freedom.

The Boasting of What He Has and Does

I was late for my flight. By the time I arrived at the gate, the plane was already backing away from the gate, getting ready for take-off. "Hey!" I yelled at the attendant. "I've got to get on that plane!"

"I'm sorry, sir," she replied politely, "but once a plane exits the boarding area there is nothing we can do. Let me try to get you on the next flight."

"I don't want the next flight!" I screamed, thinking of my plans for the weekend being disrupted. "I want this flight. It's important!"

She looked at me for a moment before asking, "How important?"

"It's a matter of life and death!" I lied.

"Yes, sir," she said, then she got on her radio and had the flight ordered back to the gate.

I'm not very proud of that moment in my life. I screamed, I lied, and I disrupted the plans of a few hundred people who were now going to be late to their destination. All because I didn't want to get home later. There was no "life and death" emergency; there was just my own pride getting in the way of my self-control. The most shocking part of my story is that I was on my return from speaking at a mayor's prayer breakfast, where I had told a thousand people about finding peace and joy in Christ. What a hypocrite! I still wonder if anyone who heard the speech at that breakfast saw my example at the airport. This is exactly the kind of thing that John warns us to stay away from in 1 John 2. Don't think of yourself as more important than you really are.

I once had an opportunity to have lunch with a professional baseball player. He was a big star, and had been outspoken about his faith in God, so I was really looking forward to meeting him. The day before our appointment, a mutual friend said to me, "You're in for the most annoying two hours of your life. That guy has read all his press clippings, and he's begun to believe them. I've never met a more arrogant Christian in my life." He was right. Rather than being regaled with interesting stories of life in the big leagues, I got to listen to this guy tell me how great he was for two full hours. It was one of the most miserable and irritating lunches of my life. But you know, I've done the very same thing!

Why is it that we feel it necessary to impress others with our credentials? Instead of bragging about ourselves, why can't we engage in a normal conversation? The answer is that we are stuck in Satan's trap. Part of his plan is to get men to believe that importance is bestowed from other men. They need to impress others so that they'll feel good about themselves. But importance doesn't come from men, it comes from God. He has given us a huge job—to do battle with Satan and win the world to Christ. Rather than trying to impress one another with our accomplishments, we are to love one another with the love of Jesus. Sharing our successes builds walls; sharing our weaknesses builds bridges. There have been times when I've found myself slipping into the pattern of thinking I'm something special, but every time I do the Lord has a way of reminding me that it's not me who is important—it's Him. God doesn't need me to work out His plan, but He has graciously allowed me to be part of it.

Occasionally I'll talk with a man who seems to think the Christian life gets easier as you get older. That's nonsense; for the godly man, it gets tougher. Forget about following any guy who tells you that his Christian walk has become easier; he has left the battle. The longer you're in it, the more effective you become and the more Satan works against you. The devil isn't pleased with having a bunch of battle-hardened veteran soldiers oppose him. He works overtime to try and get you to fail, and it becomes tougher because the flesh gets weaker as you get older. I used to be able to work all night; now if I work all night I feel it for two weeks. I like to think I'm wiser than I was twenty years ago, but I'm certainly not stronger. My weakened flesh allows me more temptation, not less. So I've got to exercise self-control if I'm going to continue as a soldier in the army of God.

Christian men wake up in these days of relative luxury, and they either start their day by thinking about envy, lust, and pride, or they start thinking about Jesus. The soldiers in the battle are thinking about the Lord. They are true to His cause. Rather than becoming addicted to the television and getting lazy, they are spending more time in the Word and getting stronger in their faith. They are patriots to the kingdom of heaven.

When the Civil War broke out, Ulysses S. Grant was at home in Galena, Illinois, working as a clerk in his father's tannery, having drunk himself out of the army three years earlier. He immediately went to Springfield to serve his country. "There are but two parties now," he said, "traitors and patriots. And I want hereafter to be ranked with the latter." That's the attitude Christ is looking for. If you are a man of self- control, God needs you in His army.

CHAPTER EIGHT

Loyal to the Cause

One of the little-known facts about the Viet Nam War was that the "Missing in Action" numbers for the U.S. Marines were always small in comparison to other service branches. The reason is that every Marine swears to be loyal to his brothers in combat. You don't leave people behind. During one battle, Marines were pinned down by the enemy. Many of us held our ground to retrieve the dead and wounded, determined not to abandon a fellow Marine. There were more soldiers killed in those retrieval actions than there had been in the original fight. The Marines who went back were loyal to the cause.

Ask yourself this question: What are you willing to die for? Every soldier has something that's important, a line in the sand that he draws. He is willing to die for the cause if he has to. In the United States, I don't believe there are many people willing to die for the faith. We've become soft, since it has historically been easy to be a Christian. Those days are ending, however. You can see it in numerous small ways; being a Christian is becoming harder and harder. We have lost the "home field advantage." Christians are mocked on television sit-coms. They are criticized in the newspaper. They are dismissed by academics, marked as "extremists" and "bigots" by left-wing political groups, and reviled by those in the media who reject the faith. Having faith in God used to be considered an important quality in a man; now it's considered a quaint exercise. Remaining sexually pure as a single adult used to be honored; now it's laughed at. Having an abortion used to be considered evil; now it's a constitutional right. It's against the law to pray in school or to hang the Ten Commandments on the schoolhouse wall, but every cult and lunatic fringe group has easy access to the student body.

The Christian purposes that are the foundation of so many of our American institutions have been whitewashed—it's hard to believe the United States government would even allow the reading of the Declaration of Independence in a federal building these days, since it contains so much talk about God. It's going to get tougher for the church, and many so-called Christians will fall away. They won't be able to handle the pressure or persecution that comes from a world that embraces Satan. They'll rationalize their decision to compromise with the world by claiming they are still Christians in their hearts, but they will no longer attend church or read their Bibles or talk about their faith. They'll be compromisers not conquerors, slackers not soldiers. At the end of time they'll be the ones saying, "Lord, didn't we do all these wonderful things in your name?" And Christ will answer, "Away from me. I never knew you" (Matthew 7:23).

A Christian soldier lets those around him see his loyalty to the cause. The apostle John makes it clear how you can recognize a Christian: You can see it in the life he leads. "If we claim to have fellowship with him yet walk in the darkness, we lie and do not live by the truth. But if we walk in the light, as he is in the light, we have fellowship with one another, and the blood of Jesus, his Son, purifies us from every sin....We know that we have come to know him if we obey his commands. The man who says, 'I know him,' but does not do what he commands is a liar, and the truth is not in him. But if anyone obeys his Word, God's love is truly made complete in him. This is how we know we are in him: Whoever claims to live in him must walk as Jesus did" (1 John 1:6-7; 2:3-6).

You can spot a Christian by the way he lives his life. The man who embraces the world and its values is of the world. The man who rejects the world to embrace the Lord belongs to God. "He who does what is right is righteous, just as he is righteous. He who does what is sinful is of the devil," John says in 1 John 3:7-8. That's the choice, and every man will be on one side or the other.

I once watched two guys meet each other at a Christian conference. They had worked at the same firm for a number of years, yet neither knew the other was a Christian. That bothers me. Everybody should be able to tell that you're a believer because of your deep love for others. They should have heard you talk about your faith. Even in a workplace antagonistic against God, you've got to reach out to people in faith. There should be no "closet Christians."

It's tough to be loyal in the face of opposition. Christ told His disciples at the Last Supper that the world would hate them, for the world hated Him. They hated Him so much that they killed Him. Now that He lives in us, they'll see that and hate us, too. That's why it takes a loyal soldier to remain strong in the faith. So if you're going to be a soldier, you're going to have to commit yourself to serving the Lord and His army. That will mean that on occasion you will be called in to help out a wounded brother.

I remember getting a call from a guy who was in deep trouble. The call came at night, after a very heavy day, and I didn't feel like going out to rescue him. But I did. He was a brother struggling in the midst of the battle, so I drove to his place and talked with him for three hours. In my mind, I was going after a wounded Marine. There are men who would come for me; they would be there to help me, or point out my stubborn sin, or offer me counsel and strength. Are there men who would come for you?

That's part of what makes us unique as soldiers of Christ. We serve a Commander who knows all about battle, but has called us to fight anyway. He has called us to be faithful in it. By relying on His power, we can reach people with His message, knock down the devil's strongholds, and defeat Satan by rescuing souls from his evil grasp. God is looking for men and women who will be loyal to Him and to each other, who will stand and fight side by side. Our protection is our faith, our mission is to share His love, and our weapon is His Spirit and Word.

We can learn a lesson from the Roman legions. A Roman guard consisted of a group of ten to twenty men, all heavily armed and trained in hand-to-hand combat. When posted to a duty, half slept while the other half kept watch. If any one man failed in his duty, he wasn't simply put to death. The entire guard was put to death, because they were to rely on one another. The authorities didn't assume that one man had failed, but that the entire company had failed. They stood by each other and fought for one another. Good soldiers today have that same attitude.

Christ said that His followers would be known for their love for one another. Paul said that the first fruit of the Spirit was love. Peter instructed us to love one another from the heart. John, in his first epistle, said that Christians will be marked by their love. He linked the obedient Christian life to the loving Christian life, and said that "anyone who claims to be in the light but hates his brother is still in the darkness" (1 John 2:9).

The world may hate you, but your fellow soldiers do not! "This is the message you heard from the beginning: We should love one another....We know that we have passed from death to life, because we love our brothers. Anyone who does not love remains in death. Anyone who hates his brother is a murderer, and you know that no murderer has eternal life in him. This is how we know what love is: Jesus Christ laid down his life for us, and we ought to lay down our lives for our brothers. If anyone has material possessions and sees his brother in need but has no pity on him, how can the love of God be in him? Dear children, let us not love with words or tongue, but with actions and in truth" (1 John 3:11-18). Christian soldiers love each other and are loyal to one another. More than anything else, that's what they are known for.

The ancient historian Josephus told a story of twelve Christians who had learned the importance of staying together. Convicted of preaching the gospel, the twelve were asked to renounce their faith and promised release if they would do so. Gathering strength from their number, they refused. Those twelve Christians were tied together, stripped of their clothing, and forced to stand together on an icy lake in the mountains. Slowly freezing to death, they huddled close to each other and began to sing. "We are twelve men together, standing for the Lord," they sang. The Roman soldiers, known for their unity, were impressed. They stayed in their barracks and listened to the bravery and faith of those Christians.

After a few hours, they noticed that the singing stopped. Soon one man, nearly frozen, stumbled into their building to squat by the fire. He had untied himself and left his friends to die, deciding to renounce his faith so as to gain a few more years of life. After a long pause, the singing voices could be heard again: "We are eleven men together, standing for the Lord," came the weak chorus. But it didn't stay weak for very long. One of the Roman soldiers, moved by a faith that caused men to surrender their lives, went running across the ice, throwing off his clothes and singing at the top of his lungs, "We are twelve men together standing for the Lord!" He chose to stand with the believers, even though it cost him his life.

When I first got into ministry, as a businessman I failed in my loyalty. I was discipling several men, and I gave up on a few of them. They were never prepared, were unfaithful, and sometimes wouldn't even show up for our meeting. So instead of sticking by them, I left them behind. I'm ashamed to admit that, for these men were potential soldiers, young Christians in training left in my care by the Lord, who is my Commanding Officer. I should have stuck by them, even when they failed. That's what Christ did. He stuck by Peter when he denied and Thomas when he doubted. But I gave up. I never want that to happen again. Now I don't hurry into a discipling relationship, but once it starts you can count on it continuing. I'm a soldier of the King, and I plan to be loyal to His purpose and people. I'll go to the wall for the men under my care.

Again, ask yourself the question: What are you willing to die for? If the answer is "nothing," you'd better hit your knees and get right with the Lord. Hard times are coming for Christians, and He's going to need some tough Christian soldiers to get through it. He needs some loyal men who are willing to sacrifice themselves, if that's what it takes, to accomplish His purposes, men who recognize that they are part of a team, leading others into battle, and who will remain loyal to the cause no matter what. He wants men who are brave, strong, and tender. Will you answer His call?

The Soldier as Model

CHAPTER NINE

The Importance of Encouragement

S oldiers are not just leaders to those around them; they also serve as models. Others look to them to find out how to act, what to do, and why it's important. A good soldier sets an example to others. He is not only strong, but brave. Others see his bravery and take courage in it. They see him prepare for battle, and that helps them know how to get ready. They see him attack the enemy's strongholds, and they follow his strategy. They are exposed to his attitude, and mimic it. They learn from watching him make war.

One of the most important tools a soldier can use in setting an example is his speech. He needs to be remain positive, using his words to encourage other soldiers. When I was first in the Marines, I had a rough time. The drill sergeants were all over me, using their words to break my will and make me tough. One particular day an instructor was on me, chewing me up one side and down the other for not getting anything right. My uniform was wrong, my boots were scuffed, my weapon handling was atrocious—he gave me the tongue-lashing of a lifetime. I was really feeling defeated, as though I'd never amount to anything. But just when I was at my lowest moment, he saw me do something right, and told me that one day I was going to make a great Marine. That single sentence completely changed my day. Suddenly I had renewed vigor, and an attitude that I could accomplish anything. Words can be remarkable tools. Mark Twain once said, "I can live for a whole week on one good compliment!"

I once talked with a woman who could verify the importance of a few encouraging words. Her daughter's husband had suddenly left her, so the mother had flown across the country to be with her daughter during the holidays. It was a rotten time, filled with both shock and sorrow. After a week of tears and prayers, the mother headed home. At the airport, she stopped into a gift shop to purchase some postcards for some grandchildren. While making small-talk with the cashier, she was asked where she was from and if she'd had a nice vacation.

Tears welled in her eyes. She explained that it had not been a vacation, but a serious family problem that had brought her across the country. She told the cashier that her daughter was having a very hard time, and that she hated to leave her alone.

That cashier stopped everything she was doing, took that mother's hand in her own and said with a warm smile, "Ma'am, God is good. He'll be with your daughter when you're not." Those simple words brought such a comfort to that worried mother that she gave the cashier a hug before moving off to catch her plane home. Words can be powerful tools for reaching out and changing the lives of people.

Paul told the believers at Ephesus, "Do not let any unwholesome talk come out of your mouths, but only what is helpful for building others up according to their needs, that it may benefit those who listen" (Ephesians 4:29). Unfortunately, it has been my experience that too many Christians use words to tear down rather than build up. They use words as negatives rather than positives, picking out everything that's wrong rather than pointing out the things that are right, and that's been too often true of me. "The mouth of the righteous is a fountain of life," Solomon said, "but violence overwhelms the mouth of the wicked. Hatred stirs up dissension, but love covers over all wrongs" (Proverbs 10:11-12).

James, the brother of Jesus Christ, recognized the trend in people to be negative, and warned, "When we put bits into the mouths of horses to make them obey us, we can turn the whole animal. Or take ships as an example. Although they are so large and are driven by strong winds, they are steered by a very small rudder wherever the pilot wants to go. Likewise the tongue is a small part of the body, but it makes great boasts. Consider what a great forest is set on fire by a small spark. The tongue also is a fire, a world of evil among the parts of the body. It corrupts the whole person, sets the whole course of his life on fire...With the tongue we praise our Lord and Father, and with it we curse men, who have been made in God's likeness. Out of the same mouth come praise and cursing. My brothers, this should not be" (James 3:3-6, 9-10).

Who has control of your tongue? How are you using it to build up others? Sister Helen Mrosla, a teacher at a Catholic school in Minnesota, told a wonderful story in an issue of Reader's Digest about using words to build up rather than to tear down. It seems she was frustrated that her third-graders were cranky and argumentative, so she instructed everyone to list their classmates on a sheet of notebook paper, then write down the nicest things they could say about each person. She took the papers home on a weekend and re-copied what everyone else had said, putting the student's name at the top of a page and listing all the nice comments from others on the sheet below. As she gave each student his or her list, the attitude of the class changed immediately. There were smiles instead of grimaces, and compliments instead of criticisms.

That's a nice idea, but the story doesn't end there. Twelve years later one of those students died in Viet Nam. At the funeral, the student's father pulled out two yellowed, worn pieces of paper—the two sheets of compliments that his son had received in Sister Mrosla's third grade class. He had taken those two pieces of paper into combat with him, and they were found on his body. That boy had treasured those positive comments for twelve years. And the amazing thing is that his boyhood friends announced that they still had their lists! One kept it at home in his top drawer. Another had it in her diary. One man had pasted it into his wedding album. And one gal waved her pieces of worn and tattered papers in the air. She kept it in her purse, a pocketful of sunshine to read during dark or depressing days. Words are powerful tools, and a good soldier knows how to use them to encourage others.

"The lips of the righteous nourish many," Solomon told his son. "The tongue of the righteous is choice silver...the lips of the righteous know what is fitting...reckless words pierce like a sword, but the tongue of the wise brings healing." His sayings and bits of inspired wisdom are replete with instructions for using words in a positive way. The wise king understood the importance words have for people. That's why he reminded his son that "a gentle answer turns away wrath," and that "he who loves a quarrel loves sin."

God's army needs some people who use their words to encourage and heal, not just to attack. Paul told his young protége, Timothy, "Keep reminding them of these things. Warn them before God against quarreling about words; it is of no value, and only ruins those who listen....Avoid godless chatter, because those who indulge in it will become more and more ungodly....Don't have anything to do with foolish and stupid arguments, because you know they produce quarrels. And the Lord's servant must not quarrel; instead, he must be kind to everyone, able to teach, not resentful. Those who oppose him he must gently instruct, in the hope that God will grant them repentance leading them to a knowledge of the truth" (2 Timothy 2:14, 16, 23-25).

It takes a mature soldier to use words that build up rather than tear down. Anyone can spot another person's problem, but it is far more difficult to recognize another's potential. Years ago I saw a performance of *Raisin in the Sun*, a play about a poor black family who inherited ten thousand dollars from the father's secret life insurance policy. The mother wants to use it to escape the ghetto of Harlem and buy a house in the country. Her daughter, a bright student, sees the money as a chance to realize her dream of attending medical school. But her son has dreams of starting a business, and he convinces his mother that his business will be an investment, reaping a harvest that will provide both a home in the country and an education for his sister. On his first day in business, his partner skips town with the ten thousand dollars, and the young man is forced to tell his family that their dream for improving their life is gone.

The daughter attacks her brother with a series of ugly epithets, calling him every name in the book. When her mother tries to cut her off by reminding her they are to love one another, the girl says, "Love him? There's nothing left to love."

With that, the mother replies, "There is always something left to love. If you ain't learned that, you ain't learned nothing. Have you cried for that boy today? I don't mean for yourself and the family because we lost all that money. I mean for him—for what he's been through and what it done to him.

Child, when do you think is the time to love somebody the most: When they done good and made things easy for everybody? Well then, you ain't through learning, because that ain't the time at all. It's when he's at his lowest and can't believe in himself, cause the world done whipped him so. When you starts measuring somebody, measure him right, child, measure him right. Make sure you done taken into account what hills and valleys he done come through before he got to wherever he is."

There are hurting Christians in this world, looking to soldiers like yourself to offer them some comfort, encouragement, and instruction. In a battle, you'll see people get wounded. You'll see people fall. When that happens, don't complain about how many are hurt, help somebody. Share some positive comments with the wounded. The daughter of a friend of mine was helping at a Special Olympics meet one time, and during the hundred-meter dash one of the participants, a retarded girl, fell down. At any other race the others would have continued on, glad to have one less competitor. But at this race the others all came over to her, helped her up, made sure she was okay, then they all started sprinting toward the finish line again. It was a beautiful picture of people more concerned about someone else's needs than their own.

Who needs your encouragement? Look around for someone in desperate need of someone to be nice to them. Say something positive. Start seeing words as your chance to share a blessing. Men in our culture have bought into an idea that we always need to be sarcastic, cutting one another down. Even in church I am continually seeing guys make "humorous" negative comments, rather than using their words to encourage others. It's time we stopped the put-downs and started some build-ups. It's time we stopped being negative and started being positive.

The nation of Israel always seemed to be using their words to complain rather than to encourage. When they were given manna, they grumbled that they didn't have meat. When they were given land, they grumbled that they didn't have their old jobs back. They were always grumbling about something, and God was always having to chastise them for turning away from Him. Grumbling, negative words take away the power of God from our lives. The most successful Christian soldiers I know are positive people. They have good things to say about their church, their pastor, and other Christians. They even have positive things to say about some very negative people. Others are drawn to them because they are positive and loving, in a negative, unloving world. "Do everything without complaining or arguing," Paul says in Philippians 2:14-16, "so that you may become blameless and pure, children of God without fault in a crooked and depraved generation, in which you shine like stars in the universe as you hold out the word of life." Positive people shine their light out to the world.

I remember our first dog. Fred loved to dig holes, so we decided we'd better put up a fence around our property. We were just getting started on that project when my neighbor came over. "No gates," he said a bit too loudly. "I don't want any gates for your dogs to come ruin my yard!"

I'd never met the guy before. His way of introducing himself was to come bark at me for putting up a fence. My initial response was anger, but the Spirit put the thought into my head: "What does that neighbor need?" He didn't need an argument, or grumbling, or even a punch in the nose. He needed Jesus Christ. So I got my kids together that night and we prayed for our neighbor's salvation. Even though their first contact with him was negative, I wanted them to start thinking positive thoughts toward this neighbor.

Some Christians seem to think they're on one side of a wall, and they're tossing gospel grenades over the wall in hopes of winning people to Christ. Their message is something like, "Jesus saves, you idiot!" But I looked at the example of Norma McCorvey, and decided there had to be another way. You remember Norma McCorvey. She was "Jane Roe" in the famous Roe vs. Wade case that legalized abortion in this country. Working for a pro-choice organization, she wasn't won to Christ by all those who screamed at her as she walked to work, jeered her at abortion rallies, or threatened her with death. She was won to Christ when the daughter of the local pro-life director made friends with her. She was won to Christ by the friendship and love she was shown by a family, even though they had serious disagreements about several lifestyle and political issues. They loved her in spite of her sin, in spite of her differences. You don't win people to Christ by beating them in an argument, but by revealing the love of God.

After my initial anger, I thought about my neighbor. He needs Jesus Christ. So Susy and I invited them over for dessert one night. We decided to build some bridges, rather than some walls. Rather than grumbling about his attitude, we started talking positively about the man. An amazing thing happened—our attitudes changed. God used that situation to change us, not him. My family is a positive team, dedicated to winning souls for Jesus Christ. We decided to get rid of the godless chatter and grumbling that are so prevalent in our world, and the Lord used our positive words to help that neighbor come down the path toward Jesus Christ.

Soldiers, your words can build or they can batter. You can encourage those around you and cause them to join you in the fight, or you can discourage them and continue fighting alone. My prayer is that you'll begin to look for ways to exercise your ability to encourage others. Christ can use our encouragement to move people into His kingdom of eternal hope and encouragement.

CHAPTER TEN

The Trustworthy Soldier

A nd the things you have heard from me in the presence of many witnesses, these entrust to faithful men who will be able to teach others also" (2 Timothy 2:2). That verse contains several truths that we'll look at, but perhaps the most interesting is that word "entrust." To entrust something to another person means to charge him with a duty, or to assign the care of something over to him for safekeeping. Paul tells Timothy that one of the roles of a Christian soldier is to entrust others with the truth. That is, help others know how to become soldiers. Set an example for them. Be a mentor for those around you.

I've heard many people talk about being "trustworthy," but most can't distinguish between trustworthiness and faithfulness. To be a trustworthy soldier means that you are dependable as an example. Others can see that you have been entrusted with the message of God, and can be counted on to reliably pass it on to others.

It's amazing to think of the trust Christ has in us. Our Lord came and spent three years with His disciples, sharing His truth and His way of life. After rising from the dead, Christ surely could have spent more time here on earth, but He chose not to. He entrusted the message of the gospel to eleven men and a few other followers. God didn't send a tract to every home, nor did He wait for an age when He could preach on television and gain a larger audience. The number of people who actually saw Jesus preach was relatively small. He entrusted the good news to eleven faithful followers, who passed on their faith to many others. Those Christians, as they came to be called, passed on their faith to still others, and so on down the line. Eventually somebody led you to the Lord. Your spiritual heritage goes back to those eleven men who had been entrusted with the gospel. Now you have been called to be a soldier and entrusted with the message of Christ. You are to keep it, guard it, and pass it along to others. It's an important trust, given by God to you.

We have attended quite a few meetings where we shared ideas that are important and helpful, but I recognize that my role as a speaker is quite limited when it comes to changing lives. I've attended some great seminars, and learned a lot from dynamic speakers, but as I ponder my beliefs, values, and ministry to reach out to men and make disciples, I find that I have been shaped more by a few significant individuals than by any seminar speaker. Teachers shared their information with me, but my mentors and spiritual parents and grandparents have shared their lives with me.

The man who discipled me not only took me into his family, he introduced me to his extended family. In doing so, Susy and I found people we didn't know, but who had been praying for us for a number of years. The woman who discipled Susy introduced us to the couple who had discipled her, and they in turn had us meet the couple who had discipled them. This was a spiritual family, and someone in that family had recommended to another that Susy and I be discipled. Our spiritual parents introduced us to our spiritual grandparents, great-grandparents, and various aunts and uncles, all of whom were part of the team effort to disciple Susy and me into maturity in Christ.

Our grandparents on Susy's side, Dave and Judy, have been tremendous models for us over the years, giving their lives to people and discipleship. Four generations back from me is an old saint named Joe, who has taught me quite a bit over the years. I would only see him two or three times over the course of a year, but each time his life greatly impacted me, as he got in my face about my relationship with the Lord, my wife, and my children. He helped me understand God's call to make disciples, and mentored me through those two or three contacts each year. The key to Joe's influence was that he and his wife, Gladys, modeled the ministry and shared it enthusiastically with younger couples in down-to-earth terms that even a former Marine could understand.

One time after an evening service Joe hollered at me from eight rows back, "Hey Phil, get out of debt!" I was incensed. Where does he get off making such a pronouncement to me in front of my family and friends? It was one of those silent trips home in the car that night, as I rehearsed the phone call I was going to make to Joe the next morning, blasting him for his lack of etiquette and sensitivity. But as I thought about it, two things stopped me. First, I had to admit that Susy and I were considering making another investment which would require borrowing more money, even though I figured it could be paid off within two years. Still, I knew that God had used Joe in profound ways on countless occasions, so there was the sliver of a possibility that God was using him to teach me. Second, I knew that this rugged old Navy Chief loved Susy and me very much, and had the courage for years to speak the truth to men whenever he felt led by the Lord.

So my call to Joe consisted of me saying thanks for his interest, and to explain my tight-jawed response to his command. To my chagrin, he didn't apologize for his public words, but simply told me again, "Phil, you need to get out of debt." It was almost two years later that I discovered why he felt so strongly: That very week Joe had submitted my name as a candidate for the role I now fill, President of Christian Business Men's Committee of USA.

Susy and I have been blessed to be surrounded by a whole family of spiritual reproducers who have loved us, forgiven us, taught us, nurtured us, warned us, and listened patiently to us, even when what was flowing from my mouth was absolute rubbish. My life would not have been the same were it not for my mentors.

There is some confusion today on the meaning of mentoring and discipleship. A narrow view of mentoring is that one person offers information to another about his career. A similar picture of discipleship is that of two people going through a biblical or spiritual course, with one serving as teacher and the other as learner. I believe both of these views are too narrow. Discipleship is more than a course, and mentoring is more than a discussion of one's career. They both refer to a mutual relationship whereby a mature man helps a protégé grow and develop. The model of Paul and Timothy perfectly describes the lifelong, mutually growing and benefitting relationship that is mentoring. The great commission of Matthew 28:19 doesn't tell us to "go therefore and make graduates of a Bible study," or to "go therefore and develop successful lawyers." Christ's commission is to "go therefore and make disciples"—soldiers for Christ. Paul told the Philippians, "But I thought it necessary to send to you Epaphroditus, my brother and fellow worker and fellow soldier..." (Philippians 2:25). Paul was a mentor to the young men around him, sharing his life and wisdom so as to help them grow.

Webster's dictionary defines mentor as "a wise, trusted adviser." He has the power to show good judgment based on his knowledge and experience, he has my confidence as a reliable person, and he shares his knowledge with me so that I can learn. A mentor doesn't just pass along information; he entrusts a message to his protégé and helps the protégé reach his full potential. It's interesting that the word mentor was originally a name. Odysseus, heading off to fight in the Trojan War, entrusted his son, Telemachus, to the care of a wise friend. That man did more than just watch the boy grow. He introduced him around, gave him an education, and developed a relationship with him so as to help him succeed. The ancient Greek's name was Mentor.

A friend of mine went to one of America's best seminaries. He learned theology, church history, and the exposition of Greek and Hebrew texts. But he didn't learn to be a pastor in seminary. He got that from spending time with his local pastor. It seems that pastor had a heart for mentoring, so he took my friend into the boardroom, to show him how an elder board worked. He took him visiting, taught him to preach, and revealed the importance of prayer. They talked together about the joys and sorrows of ministry, and would often critique the worship services to see how they could improve. Just as important as the seminary classes was the real-world experience of how to pastor. A man can make a more significant impact on this world for the cause of Christ by investing in

fewer people. Our world says that if a man wants to be important, he ought to spend time with the masses, but if you'll look
at the biblical account of Jesus Christ you will find that as time
went on He spent less time with the masses and more time
with the twelve.

The process of mentoring dates back to the earliest of
times, when fathers taught their sons the family trade. Joseph
taught Jesus how to be a carpenter, and the Lord worked at it
until He began His public ministry. Master craftsmen have
always had apprentices to whom they could pass on not only
their secrets and skills, but their diligence, honesty, and pride
in their work. Leonardo Da Vinci mentored Michelangelo.
Franz Haydn mentored Ludwig Van Beethoven. Leo Tolstoy
mentored Boris Pasternak. The leaders of today have always
taken care to prepare the leaders of tomorrow. The best sur-
geons in the world were once unskilled interns who were
mentored into the finer points of surgery. Plumbers and car-
penters still use mentoring programs, as do some jewelers and
teachers.

Unfortunately, there aren't that many Christians who are
mentoring and discipling—a fact that scares me. If Christ gave
us that as an example to follow, I fear we abandon His meth-
ods at our peril. Every man who wants to become a soldier
ought to have a mentor. You can't get all the information you
need to know from a class or a book; you need a personal relationship with an experienced Christian.

When I was training to be a soldier, I was mentored by
those with experience in soldiering. They smelled of battle.
Those who knew how to be tough, how to be brave, and how
to be dangerous in battle entrusted to me the secrets and skills
of successful soldiering. When I arrived as a raw recruit
machine gunner, straight from training, I was assigned to the
Second Battalion, Fifth Marines, and into the care of an experienced machine gun team leader named Ralph. There I was, a

pampered, middle-class white kid, sitting in a life-and-death unit of the "Fighting Fifth Marines." The sergeant pointed me in the direction of a bald, mustached black man, covered with diesel fuel and cleaning his weapon from the latest battle. He didn't even look up. I took one look at Ralph, who was built like an ox, and I felt like writing home to Mom and asking for a sick pass.

This guy was tough as nails. I figured it would be best if I just shut up, learned my job, and tried to learn what this guy knew, because he'd been through combat and survived with great courage. After several ambushes and search-and-destroy missions, Ralph and I became inseparable. He was the best machine gunner in our outfit, and through his teaching I rapidly became the second best. Ralph had flunked out of the University of Michigan, and I'd flunked out of Ohio University, so we used to joke that he and I were the only guys in our squad who knew that Oedipus Rex was not a venereal disease!

About a month later, we were headed up a burned part of a mountain in the northern highlands of South Viet Nam, when we encountered an enemy column. It was one of the very few times we surprised the enemy. Not wanting to lose the element of surprise, we didn't take cover but simply opened fire on the enemy column in the valley below. They returned fire, and after about a hundred rounds in the first few seconds of combat, Ralph's machine gun jammed. For the next minute or so, which seems like a year in combat, Ralph and I stood together in a clearing on a hill, automatic weapon fire popping all around our heads and shoulders, dismantling the rear assembly of the machine gun. We cleared it, put it back together again, and got it up and firing. There is no experience among men greater than standing together with courage in the midst of combat, saving each other's skin. Ralph and I were never the same after that day, because we knew without a shadow of a doubt that we could depend on each other for our lives.

The outfit learned something that day, too, which always resulted in their wanting our machine gun team to go with them on their missions. When I became a Christian, the same process took place. Those mature in the faith took the time to share their lives with me and show me how to be brave with the gospel, how to be strong in the faith, and how to be tender with people. They entrusted to me the ministry of being a soldier in the army of God. No one left me to simply read the books. They shared their lives with me, and I was changed because of these relationships. In the discipleship realm, there have been men and women who stood with Susy and me in life and death situations, like my father's suicide or the birth of our children. They've stood with us as we faced disappointment at the turns God has allowed to happen in our lives.

The next generation of Christians needs you to disciple and mentor them. They need to be established in the faith, entrusted with the message of the gospel, and trained to mobilize other men for disciple-making. They need a model to follow, an experienced friend who can take them through a practical, hands-on time of training. They need someone to take them under his wing and share wisdom with them—a coach to help them learn from their failures; a loving uncle to plainly tell them the facts of life. Too many Christians are merely getting head-knowledge these days, and what they need is a caring, wise adviser.

Susy and I were not merely taught, we were "parented" by an extended family who didn't merely impart information, but shared their very lives. They followed the example mentioned by the apostle Paul in 1 Thessalonians 2:7-8: "But we proved to be gentle among you, as a nursing mother tenderly cares for her own children. Having thus a fond affection for you, we were well-pleased to impart to you not only the gospel of God but also our own lives, because you had become very dear to us."

The concept of spiritual parenting has become a critical part of our process at CBMC. We believe there are two stages to the evangelism-discipleship process. The first stage is farming, where the believer is cultivating his relationships with non-believers, sowing seeds of the gospel, and harvesting new souls for the kingdom of God. The second stage is parenting, where the discipler is helping the new Christian grow into Christ-likeness. That new believer will move through spiritual infancy, become a child in the faith, then move through an adolescent faith before becoming a spiritually mature adult. Operation Timothy, the discipleship tools we have developed to assist this maturing process, was significant in my own spiritual walk. As my spiritual father and I worked through the lessons on forgiveness and acceptance, I began to really understand what becoming a Christian was all about. As we explored the role of the Holy Spirit and practical ways to overcome temptation, I started seeing positive progress in my spiritual walk. Then as we examined how to integrate Christ's principles into my home and workplace, seeing the world God's way and multiplying my life through others, I moved toward maturity in Christ. I'm not totally there yet, of course, but the process of discipleship has caused me to grow in my faith and practice.

Perhaps our new-found mobility has disrupted the process. Many of us grew up moving from place to place, hundreds of miles from our extended families, separated from those uncles and godparents who could have helped us grow up. Consequently, most American men don't have a relationship with anyone who could be a mentor. They wonder if there is anyone who really cares for them. They feel relationally disconnected from everyone. Think of the impact you can have by entrusting the principles of soldiering to them, and becoming that person to whom they can go for advice and encouragement and hands-on spiritual training for the battle.

A friend called this morning, a man who has been a Christian for twenty years. He had just returned from a Promise Keepers conference, and told me he needed help on two issues: His work and his family. He said to me, "Phil, I know a lot of people, but you are the only one to whom I am close enough to ask tough questions. You're really the only close friend I have." We all need somebody to whom we can turn for advice.

What difference would it have made to you if, when you were twenty-one, someone older whom you respected had come up to you and said something like this: "You know, I've been watching you. You have a lot of ability. I'd like to see you succeed. What if we were to meet together once in a while to talk about life?" Most of us would have jumped at the chance.

One of our greatest challenges, yet one of our greatest blessings, has been to meet with groups of young couples to talk about their relationships with God and each other. We meet two or three times a year for highly intense, personal accountability. One of the men told me on the phone the other day, "Phil, I don't know what I'd do without you as my mentor." I quickly responded, "No, Scott, you are mentoring me. For you see, when we get together to share experiences from our different perspectives, I learn from a younger gener-ation, which has a much better grasp on relationships and intimacy than my own generation."

Our encounters often include "the hot seat," a time when one man or one couple sit in the middle of a circle while the others in the group ask them about their spiritual walk. Sometimes I'll be in the center of that circle for three hours! I might be able to lie for an hour, but these guys are serious about my walk with God and whether I'm keeping my com-mitment to Susy, so eventually we get to the truth. "Okay,

Phil," Scott said to me once as I was sitting in the hot seat, "get out your calendar and show us where you've scheduled time away with your wife, without the kids." I mean, these guys are tough, and they won't cut me any slack. They aren't impressed by my position or our organizational structure; they're concerned about serving the Lord faithfully and being my friends. These are guys with whom I'm going to war; guys I can depend on and who depend on me.

I know that meeting with people and investing in them takes time, but there is no greater joy than seeing your spiritual children walking with God. As the apostle John said, "I have no greater joy than this, to have my children walking in the truth" (3 John 4). Students are looking for somebody who can teach them more than they can read in books. Newly married people are anxious to have someone share with them an example of a fulfilling marriage. Those getting started in their careers long for a more experienced hand to help guide them.

When I was just out of high school, I decided to attend Ohio University in Athens, Ohio. My father had been student body president there, my grandfather taught English at the school, and I could count seventeen relatives who had graduated from the school, so I figured I was all set. Unfortunately, nobody told me I had to go to classes and study. (Or, if they did tell me, I wasn't paying attention.) I had no model to follow, nor any accountability. There was no one to mentor me through college. I was given the boot, and a year later I wound up in the Marine Corps. I was immediately made a machine gunner—a position which, at that time, had the shortest life expectancy of any combat position. I loved the idea of being in battle. The exhilaration and heroism made me think I was John Wayne.

I was in Viet Nam about two weeks when I found out that John Wayne had lied. In November of 1967 my company led a helicopter assault at dawn. We dropped from the skies, then tried to run across an open rice field in what was supposed to be a surprise attack, only to find an entrenched enemy. We lost a third of our company in the first ninety seconds. Men were dropping all around me. We called in bombers, but they couldn't help us because we were literally nose to nose with the Viet Cong. At noon, under heavy attack, my company was ordered to charge the left flank. That's the day I passed my machine gun to my best friend, John, then watched him die in my place. I experienced unbelievable pain. As we put John's body onto the chopper, I realized his new bride would never see him again. He'd been married two weeks before coming over, and his wife had just written to say that she was pregnant. John would never see that baby. I'd had mentors in the military, but none with whom I could talk about the hurt.

When I got back to the states, no college would let me in. Even the junior colleges turned me down because of my past academic performance. Then a brand new institution opened up that must have been desperate for students. I got in, received good grades, and was able to get accepted into Southern Methodist University. That's where I met Susy. We married, then moved to Atlanta to attend Emory School of Law. After graduation, Susy became a corporate attorney for Delta Air Lines and I became the first new lawyer at a firm that was about to experience significant growth. That's when I found out that John Wayne had lied again. Success and money didn't bring joy and peace of mind like they did in the movies.

My marriage looked good on the outside, but our relationship was a disaster. I found that my reputation in the courtroom was only as good as my last case. We joined a church—I even taught Sunday School!—but I had no peace. There was a ton of pressure on me, and I brought all my anxiety and fear home to my wife. My temper would get out of control. There were blow ups and broken furniture. I apparently had the great American dream, but the dream had let me down. Then one day I went to hear a CBMC speaker. He was a general contractor, and I was suing a general contractor at that time, so I thought I might get some useful information. I was right. His life and his struggles got my attention. I was looking for peace and he told me I could find it in Jesus Christ. I found out God knows me and loves me. He loves me so much that He sent His Son to die for me.

I knew I had sinned and broken God's law, but I was trying to live as though there was no penalty for sin. "The wages of sin is death," Paul says in Romans 6:23, "but the gift of God is eternal life through Jesus Christ our Lord." I was spiritually dead, separated from God by my sin. I was going to face judgment from God for all the sins I had committed in this life. But then I was told a wonderful truth: "But God demonstrates His own love toward us, in that while we were yet sinners, Christ died for us" (Romans 5:8).

Jesus paid the penalty for my sins when He died on the cross. The apostle Peter put it this way: "For Christ also died for sins once for all, the just for the unjust, in order that He might bring us to God" (1 Peter 3:18). I had always thought I could do enough good things in my life to outweigh the bad, and that would get me into heaven. But I was never sure how to do good things. I kept doing bad things, and this man told me all my good works would never save me anyway. He quoted from Ephesians 2:8-9, "For by grace you have been saved through faith; and that not of yourselves, it is the gift of God; not as a result of works, that no one should boast." My good works wouldn't get me into heaven, but faith in Jesus Christ would. As He said, "He who hears my word and believes Him who sent me, has eternal life, and does not come into judgment, but has passed out of death into life" (John 5:24).

I discovered that there is no other way to God. "I am the way, the truth, and the life," Jesus says in John 14:6. "No one comes to the Father except through me." So I took notes, thought about what he said, and several months later accepted Christ as my personal Savior.

A physician began meeting with me in a weekly one-on-one Bible study that is Operation Timothy, and he began discipling me. He showed me how to grow in Christ, how to treat my wife, and how to be a soldier. He entrusted to me the truths of the faith, and gave me a heart for passing it along to others. When I asked him one time why he was willing to invest so much time and energy into my life, he told me it was because someone else had done it for him. He was just another link in the chain between the original disciples and myself. Now I'm taking the truths of God and entrusting them to others.

We need to be producing reproducers. We need to be passing on our lives to the next generation, so like in Isaiah 60:22, one will become a thousand. A mentor entrusts to his protégé knowledge that would be difficult to learn on one's own. He teaches the protégé what he'll need to know to be successful in life. Rich DeVos, the founder of the Amway Corporation, calls the mentor the "keeper of traditions." That is, he knows the stories and secrets that are important to pass along. The mentor is available, ready to listen, ready to ask questions. He advises, confronts, and teaches. He believes in the potential of the protégé, and tells him.

It's been my experience that most Christian men want to disciple someone else, but don't feel qualified to do so. As a soldier, if you are farther down the path of spiritual maturity than someone else, you can disciple him. What it takes is a heart for people and a willingness to share your example with others. A soldier is a model, and he can learn to explain that model to someone else. He can entrust the workings of that model to another person. Mentoring and discipleship are the keys to unlocking the potential of seventy-five percent of all men in the church. They are just waiting for someone to come along beside them and help them grow. They are waiting for a *relationship* that will help them grow.

Most Christian men need help with their family life. They're unsure about their role as husband and father, especially if they come from a single-parent or a non-Christian home. The average guy doesn't know how to cultivate a relationship with his wife. He needs help in being a godly example to his kids. Another man willing to invest in his life can entrust him with stories, ideas, and principles for fostering a great marriage. That's what changed my marriage. Susy was ready to divorce me, but our love was rekindled when my life changed. When you look at the divorce rate in this country, you can imagine the significant impact your good marriage can have on the lives of those around you.

Most Christian men also need help with their financial lives. It's been my experience that money is a continuing problem for Christians. They need help in knowing how to think about money, how to budget, how to spend, and how to use it to God's glory. You can entrust those around you with God's principles for finances. Operation Timothy is a cutting-edge study covering topics such as forgiveness, assurance, temptation, Bible study, prayer, God's will, handling money, and many other important issues. It's a great resource for bringing another man toward maturity in Christ.

Obviously, you can help men grow in their faith. As you entrust the principles for a solid spiritual life to others, you'll begin creating new soldiers for the kingdom. Our churches are full of men and women who know the truth of God's Word, but who never do anything about it. They enjoy the music, take notes on the sermon, and participate in a Sunday School class or a home Bible study, but they don't know how to take their faith beyond the doors of the church. As a Christian soldier, you're going to help them see how their faith influences everything about their lives. It shapes their lifestyle choices, their conversation, their friendships, and their careers. They'll start to understand the war that is going on between God and Satan—a war that is neglected by too many of God's people.

You can help others recognize the war and what each person can do in the battle. Every Christian has a role to play, and the reason we seem to be losing the cultural war in America is because not enough Christians have recognized the war and gone on the offensive. We are not here to defend institutions, but to assault the enemy and free his captives with the love of Christ. Jesus is the center of who we are, and all relationships and activities flow out of Him. The focus of our lives should be evangelism and discipleship.

Men also need help with their feelings. Mentors can help protégés understand how to stay emotionally healthy, personally fulfilled, and intellectually balanced. Many struggle with concerns about success and significance, and are unsure as to the meaning of life. A mentor can entrust to a protégé the purpose that comes from the Lord Jesus, the only One in the world who offers true meaning. Rather than chasing property, power, or position, he can learn to chase after the one thing that will bring satisfaction in this life: Peace with God.

Another area where you can assist many men is in the area of friends. Because our society has stressed the "Lone Ranger" mentality for so long, men have become relationally disconnected. A mentor can help connect people, and can build a lifelong relationship that fosters other healthy relationships. If you entrust to others the importance of friendship and accountability, those around you will value their relationships.

To become good soldiers, men will also need help with their fitness. That is, they'll need to get in shape for the battle. There are millions of men who need help to get in shape physically. A man might not do it on his own, but if he has your example to follow, he is much more likely to lose the weight and shape up. God needs men who are hardened warriors for the battle. The only way most men will choose to become physically strong is by following the example of their leaders.

Finally, you won't be able to completely touch men's lives unless you talk about their jobs—their functions. If you can entrust to them a biblical concept of work, helping them to see how God is using them to fight the war, you'll be shaping soldiers for the battle. All of these things—family, finances, faith, feelings, friends, fitness, and function—can be shaped by a discipler.

These are the seven basic areas that affect all men. You must first make sure either that those are areas of strength in your own life, or that you have analyzed your weaknesses and are working on them. Then you can begin entrusting to men the principles for success in each area. Evangelism and discipleship is the core, out of which come all of our other activities. Susy knows that she and I are a team, evangelizing and discipling our children, our friends, and our neighbors. We're discipling one another, mentoring one another, keeping one another accountable, and helping our children understand that their entire lives are to be used to move people toward the Lord Jesus Christ. Susy and I are in ministry with one another, enriching one another's lives through our relationship with God. Again, you don't have to be perfect. You just need to be able to set an example of maturity in each area. The people around you are watching your example, and they are waiting for someone to help them succeed. America is facing a lack of leadership, and mentoring helps to put people into leadership by entrusting them with the greatest assignment—changing the world.

CHAPTER ELEVEN

Faithful in All Things

Take another look at 2 Timothy 2:2: "And the things which you have heard from me in the presence of many witnesses, these entrust to faithful men, who will be able to teach others also." Paul tells his young charge not only that he is to entrust the things of God to others, but that he is to choose faithful men. The word can also be translated "reliable". We don't always look for faithful men when choosing soldiers. Most of us have a tendency to focus on flashier skills. I think it's interesting that Paul mentioned the importance of faithfulness before mentioning their ability to teach. You see, being able to get up front and speak is a great skill to have, but it can cover a shallow faith. We've all seen men and women who can "wow" a crowd with a great story, but when you get to know them you discover they aren't real. Their "up front" ability has eclipsed their "down low" reliability. Still, we're drawn to those who have charisma over those who have conviction. Our world loves style more than substance.

A friend of mine is a pastor in a large church, and he has a great method for gauging the faithfulness of those who want to be pastors. He had read that The Navigators always started staff people with scrubbing floors, so when approached by a young man looking for an internship, he invariably tells the potential pastor, "Great! We've got some important work you can do for us." Then he asks the man to scrub the toilets. He tells me he has seen every response imaginable. Some have gotten angry, others have acted offended, and still others have simply walked away. But some will take the brush and go do the work. He isn't trying to demean anyone, but he wants to see if the person is really willing to do whatever it takes to get into ministry. Besides, a lot of pastoral ministry consists of cleaning up after the messes of others!

My friend told me that he once had two young men begin attending his church about the same time. Both were interested in the opening for youth intern. One guy was tall and handsome, with an ability to sing. Unfortunately, he was a conceited jerk. The kids in the youth group were impressed with his smoothness, but no one could get close to him. When the pastor asked him to clean the toilets, he acted as though he'd been slapped in the face. He was much too good to be wasting his talent on toilet scrubbing. The pastor, noting that Christ didn't find Himself too low to wash feet, thanked the young man for coming in and dismissed him.

The other candidate was a guy, without a great public persona but with a real heart for God. When the pastor asked him to scrub toilets, he simply picked up the brush and headed off for the nearest stall. He proved himself faithful, and it led to a position in the church. The young man was a diamond in the rough, and he ended up having a wonderful ministry in the lives of many youths.

Christ, in telling the parable of the talents, said that we would each be held accountable for what God has given us. To those who have much ability, much is required. To those who have little, little is required. But we are all responsible to prove ourselves faithful. Elders in the early church were not to be new converts, but men who had shown themselves faithful over time. They had kept the faith, been loyal to Christ, and had revealed their sense of duty through their conscientiousness and dependability. A soldier in the army of God needs to set an example of faithfulness, so that others around can see his example and take courage during the battle.

Think of how encouraged you are when you see someone remaining loyal in the face of strong opposition. You've got to love the example of Peter and John, who, when beaten for preaching the gospel, rejoiced that they were counted worthy of suffering for the sake of Christ. That sort of faithfulness inspires others.

Warfare often brings out the best in men. In World War I, the story is told of an American GI who watched a brave German soldier get wounded in a narrow no-man's-land between two trenches. After listening to him scream, that American crawled out to his enemy. Upon seeing what was happening, first one side, then the other, ceased firing. The American made his way to the German soldier, disentangled him from the barbed wire, took him in his arms, and walked toward the German trenches to leave him in the hands of his comrades. Having done so, he turned to start back to his own lines, but a hand reached out and spun him around. The German officer who had grabbed him was wearing an Iron Cross, the highest German honor for bravery. He pulled it from his own uniform and placed it on the American, who then walked back to his own side of the battle. God is looking for faithful soldiers to fight in the battle.

Years ago I read an interview with Mother Theresa, who for many years has worked with the poorest of the poor in India. When asked if she was discouraged because so many of the people she works with die, she replied, "No, for God has not called me to a ministry of success. He has called me to a ministry of mercy." I love that! She understands that we are to be faithful to God, even when we don't see the splendor and success our society demands.

I once spent three years of my life discipling a guy who just didn't seem to take it seriously. We would meet every week at the same time, and he was always late. He would still forget our meetings after they'd been going on for two years. Did I waste my time? Some would think so, since that guy never did get his life together. But God hasn't called me to be successful; He's called me to be faithful. It's God who determines what "success" is. Over the last twenty years, for every guy who has flaked out on me I've got ten who have moved on and become strong soldiers in the faith. Don't assume that just because you are faithful everything is going to go your way.

When Susy and I were called to join the ministry of CBMC, we were faithful to the call. I had an income from my law firm, and we had a very expensive home in Atlanta that we planned to sell. What we didn't count on was the law firm splitting up after my leaving, or the home taking almost five years to sell. Suddenly our great income sources were gone. Did that mean we were making a mistake? Had we misread God's intention for us? No, the Lord simply wanted to know if we were going to remain faithful. We needed to learn some valuable lessons. It's easy to have faith in God's provision when you've got a pile of money in the bank. It's much more difficult when all your money disappears. So we learned to rely on God, and He built our faith.

When Paul was on his first missionary journey, he had along with him a young man named John Mark. During the course of their work, John Mark abandoned Paul and Barnabas, perhaps out of fear and discouragement. Ashamed, he went home. Paul must have been deeply hurt by John Mark's actions, for some time later, when Paul and Barnabas were preparing to go on another mission trip, the topic of John Mark came up. Barnabas, ever the encourager, wanted to take John Mark along. Paul would have none of it. The two friends argued so vehemently that they parted company. Acts chapter fifteen says that Barnabas took John Mark and sailed for Cyprus, while Paul found a new partner, Silas, and left for Syria.

Paul wanted to give up on John Mark, for he had not shown himself faithful. But that story offers an ending that gives hope to all those who have ever run from the battle. John Mark proved himself faithful this time. Even though he's failed before, this time he came through. Paul began to believe in him again, and late in his life, Paul asked for John Mark to join him, saying, "He is useful to me for service" (2 Timothy 4:11). John Mark became a faithful soldier because Barnabas believed in him, and demonstrated his own faithfulness in sticking by him. Eventually John Mark wrote one of the books of Scripture—the Gospel of Mark.

We need to be faithful men, training other men to be faithful, and reaching out to others in the battle. I have been blessed to have faithful men in my life. I have one friend who calls me regularly, not to check on the ministry, but just to ask me how I'm doing personally. He prays for me, and I know that he cares about me. He is always asking, "Is there anything I can do for you?" I appreciate his faithfulness. Sometimes he is the only man in my life asking, "How are you doing?" Faithfulness is one of the marks of a brave soldier.

Stu Weber tells a wonderful story of a soldier who was wounded in battle, and his friend came out to get him. The commanding officer tried to stop him, calling it a suicide mission, but that soldier was not about to let his best friend die without doing all he could to help him. He crawled onto the field of battle, under heavy fire, and brought his friend back to safety. Unfortunately, his friend had died from his wounds. The officer, barking at him for putting himself in harm's way, asked, "Well, soldier, he's dead. Do you think it was worth the risk?"

The soldier, still holding his friend's body, replied, "Yes, sir, it was. You see, he was still alive when I got to him. His last words were, I knew you'd come.'" A faithful soldier does what he knows is right, even if it's hard. Even if it looks like a failure. We're not all called to succeed, but we are all called to be faithful.

A friend of mine once had an opportunity to meet Ivory Crocket, a man who came from poverty to become a world-class sprinter in the 1970's. My friend, a sprinter himself in college, asked Mr. Crocket what it would take to reach his level. His answer: "To become the best at anything takes three things: Vision, passion, and integrity." What a classic response!

If you want to be a faithful soldier, you must first have vision. What is it God is calling you to do? For what do you have a vision? I have a vision for training tens of thousands of men to be soldiers for Christ. Our vision statement at Christian Business Men's Committee is this: Impacting the world by saturating the business and professional community with the Gospel of Jesus Christ, by establishing, equipping, and mobilizing teams where we work and live that yield spiritual reproducers. What is your vision?

One man can do incredible things with a strong vision. Bill Bright started Campus Crusade for Christ because he had a vision for winning young people to Christ. Dawson Trotman began The Navigators because he had a vision for discipling men in the Navy. Steve Jobs and Steve Wosniak created the first home computer in their garage because they had a vision for taking technology and putting it on every desk in the country. God has placed in your heart a desire to do certain things, and they are uniquely different from those of any other person. Your vision might be small or grand, but you've got to know what it is if you expect to put it into practice. Solomon told us in Proverbs that where there is no vision, the people perish. If you could accomplish anything for God, what would it be? What has He given you a heart for? What is your vision? In formulating your vision, remember that only the Word of God and the souls of people last forever.

DeWitt Wallace had a vision for a new sort of magazine that would collect the best writings from other publications and put them in one easy package for readers. He talked with a number of publishers, but they all turned him down. Still, DeWitt believed in his idea, so he started sending letters to potential subscribers. The response was overwhelmingly positive, and today Reader's Digest is the most popular magazine in the world.

Sprinters have a saying: "Keep your eyes on the prize." That is, when you're running in your lane, you keep your eyes focused on the finish line. If you look at your opponents, the movement of your head will slow you down. If you look at the track, the motion of your head will cause your stride to shorten. So you keep your eyes on the prize: The tape stretched across the finish line. We need to do the same thing. Keep your mind focused on your vision. Soldier, what is God calling you to do?

The second principle Ivory Crocket gave for being your best is to have passion. You've got to want to succeed very badly. Every four years we celebrate the Olympics, which features men and women who are passionate about one thing. A shot-putter has tossed that sixteen-pound ball again and again, going over every little nuance to improve his technique. He has put in hours and hours toward one goal: Winning the Olympics. And of course, there are a host of others competing against him who have the same goal. They can't all win, but they can all be faithful to do their best.

I find a lack of passion in Christian circles today. Prayer meetings have died out, and nobody wants to believe in hell any more because it's too inconvenient. But winning a war requires people of passion. Ted DeMoss, my predecessor, was president of CBMC for thirteen years. He has devoted his life to reaching men before they reach hell. He likes to ask three questions: Do we believe what the Bible says about hell? Do we believe that those without Christ are going there? And do we care?

William Booth, the founder of the Salvation Army, once said he wished he could give every one of his people one hour in hell, so that they could see what misery the lost were bound for if they did not accept Jesus Christ. That's passion. Paul spoke of athletes going into strict training to win crowns that did not last, but Christians have been given an opportunity to earn a crown that will last forever. We ought to be known for our passion—passion for God, passion to defeat Satan, passion to win others to the Lord, and passion to produce reproducers. Paul says in 1 Corinthians 15:58, "Always give yourselves fully to the work of the Lord, knowing that your labor for the Lord is not in vain." Even when you think you're going through a pointless exercise, God is using you. Be faithful to Him, for faithful men are men of passion. "Do not become weary in doing good," Paul tells the Galatians in chapter six, verse nine, "for at the proper time we will reap a harvest if we do not give up." Faithful men don't give up. They remain bravely fighting for the Lord.

I love Paul's challenge in Colossians 3:23: "Whatever you do, work at it with all your heart, as working for the Lord, not for men." You aren't working for your boss, you are serving the King! At a CBMC breakfast I heard a man say that, when interviewing candidates for his business, he always liked to ask the question, "What's your purpose in life?" He told us recently that when he had asked a young man that question, he got this response: "My purpose in life is to go to heaven, and take as many people with me as I can." Now there is a man of passion.

Paul wrote to the Christians at Philippi and told them about his passion. He was in chains for preaching the gospel, and he had heard that others were criticizing his style. But rather than letting it get him down, he said, "It is true that some preach Christ out of envy and rivalry, but others out of good will. The latter do so in love, knowing that I am put here for the defense of the gospel. The former preach Christ out of selfish ambition, not sincerely, supposing that they can stir up trouble for me while I am in chains. But what does it matter? The important thing is that in every way, whether from false motives or true, Christ is preached. And because of this, I rejoice" (Philippians 1:15-18). Paul's vision was to take the gospel to the world, and he had the passion to rejoice even when it caused him pain. There's a guy drunk on the Holy Spirit!

The story of Elijah is one filled with passion. I love reading about the prophet of God challenging the pagans to a contest. Do you remember the story, in 1 Kings 18, when everybody went to the top of Mount Carmel and built a big altar? The pagans prayed to their god, but nothing happened. Elijah, who apparently had a sense of humor, suggested their god must be asleep, so they should yell louder. Those pagans screamed and cut themselves and danced about, but nothing ever happened. Then it was Elijah's turn. However, rather than praying, he had the people dump water on the sacrifices, so that no one could look back later and claim it was the spark from a pagan deity that really lit that bonfire. Then he had them dump water on it again, then a third time. Then that man of God prayed that the Lord would reveal Himself to the people, and fire cascaded down from heaven and burned up the sacrifices. The thing that gets me most about that wonderful account is the passion of Elijah. It took some real guts to make that challenge, and it took tremendous faith to have water poured on the altar. But Elijah was a faithful man, a man of vision and passion. He set an example for everyone to follow, and rekindled faith in God among his people. As Solomon said, "Where there is no vision, the people perish."

When I look back on the statement Ivory Crocket made to my friend, I'm glad that he added "integrity" to the list. Men of faith maintain their integrity. It's too easy for someone to claim they have a great message from God when they don't have the lifestyle of someone belonging to the Lord. In recent years we've watched countless prominent Christians, both men and women, lose their integrity in very public ways. Hebrews 13:7 warns us that we'll all have to give an accounting for our lives, and some people are going to be disqualified. If you really want to make an impact in the spiritual war, be holy. The prophet Daniel, told he couldn't pray to God, openly disobeyed the law. He prized his integrity over his own life. People will respond to a man of integrity. Without it, no one will look to your example. You won't be able to influence anyone. With it, you'll prove yourself faithful to the cause.

The first-century Christians were warriors in the spiritual battle. They banded together and in the face of stiff opposition took a strong stand for Christ. A quick look at that group of people reveals a faithful army. "They devoted themselves to the apostles' teaching and to the fellowship, to the breaking of bread and to prayer. Everyone was filled with awe, and many wonders and miraculous signs were done by the apostles. All the believers were together and had everything in common. Selling their possessions and goods, they gave to anyone as he had need. Every day they continued to meet together in the temple courts. They broke bread in their homes and ate together with glad and sincere hearts, praising God and enjoying the favor of all the people. And the Lord added to their number daily those who were being saved" (Acts 2:42-47).

Look at the character of those Christians. They were redeemed. Their lives were changed. They were loving and unified. Others looked with awe at the spiritual power they displayed, and they appreciated the ministry. These were clearly the people of God, bent on changing the order of things in this world. In the face of government and social opposition, they were faithful to the truth.

Now look at the consequences of their lives. These Christians experienced gladness and joy in a largely unhappy world. Their love attracted others to the faith. They brought in new people and trained them to be soldiers for Christ. Their vision for winning the lost, passion for God, and personal integrity were evident in everything they did. These were people of faith. We are called to be like them—faithful to the cause, no matter what the circumstances.

Soldier, what's your vision? Where is your passion? Are you maintaining your integrity? If we are going to win this battle, we need to have soldiers who are faithful in all things.

CHAPTER TWELVE

Teaching and Being Teachable

There is one more element of 2 Timothy 2:2 that needs to be explored, and it is one that is often overlooked. "And the things which you have heard from me in the presence of many witnesses, these entrust to faithful men, who will be able to teach others also." The ability to teach is imperative for a soldier. If you are expecting to recruit others into God's army and lead them into battle, you're going to have to be able to teach. If you can't communicate what you believe, you'll never be able to lead anyone else to Christ. And if you aren't willing to learn how to communicate your faith, you don't have a heart for the unsaved.

The fact is, you are an example to others. As a soldier, they are looking to you, to see how you do things. If you cannot articulate your belief in God and the story of your relationship to Him, you'll never take your place as a kingdom warrior. It takes a brave man to talk about his faith, particularly in a world that denigrates Christianity and holiness. You've got to decide if you can be brave, not just strong.

When I was in the Marine Corps, my commanding officer had me break down my machine gun in the dark. On more than one occasion he ordered me to sleep with it in my bunk. He knew if I could break something down into its basic parts and live with it, I'd be able to use it effectively. The more time I spent with it, the better I knew that weapon. That's what we've got to do with our faith. If we can think through what we believe, and be able to talk calmly and coherently about it, God can use us to reach others. As Paul said to Philemon, "I pray that you may be active in sharing your faith, so that you will have a full understanding of every good thing we have in Christ." You'll understand your faith better the more you talk about it.

There are plenty of Christians today who have biblical knowledge, but few with the guts and transparency to share it. They take classes and read books, but they never get around to saying the words of the gospel to someone else. It reminds me of the baseball clinic my boys attended. They were told all about the finer points of pitching at the clinic, but as soon as the game started they forgot all that they'd learned. To become a better pitcher, you have to practice. Some pitches require a unique, almost unnatural motion, so to throw it means retraining your muscles to work in a new way. That will only come with practice.

I've found that a great way to share your faith is to pack it around a felt need. For example, the man in the office next to you or your neighbor next door is probably struggling with stress over his job, finances, wife, children, or health. When you come alongside and mention similar stress in your own life, it's natural for him to pick up on your transparency, feel safe with you, and share something touching him deeply at that time. By building a relationship with him, you can move him toward the true answer to his problems naturally and in an unforced way.

On an airplane recently the man next to me asked me what I did for a living. Instead of giving him a job title, I told him that I'm involved with men around the country who are working alongside men in the marketplace struggling with stress and uncertainty. That phrase almost always begins an in-depth conversation into a man's life. If you want to be sharing your faith, you've got to practice saying the words. It will seem unnatural at first. I always felt like there was a big "thud" every time I brought up the words of the gospel with someone. There would be this sort of awkward silence, and I was sure I'd breached some rule of etiquette. I had to learn to make God part of my normal conversation, and that took time. I knew that just sitting in church wasn't enough. I had to have some training.

I know someone who works for the Drug Enforcement Agency. He spent months at Quantico, learning how to spot smugglers and what to do in an interdiction. Then he was assigned to the Miami area. One day he was at the airport, working on a tip from an informant, with a drug-sniffing dog at his side. Two guys walked by with their luggage, and the drug dog barked. Before he knew what he was doing, the agent had pulled his weapon and was pointing it at the suspects. You see, when danger came he didn't have to think—his training took over. That's where we need to be in our own spiritual battle. Be so prepared to talk about your faith that, in a conversation, you don't have to stop and gear up to talk about God.

Think it through beforehand so that when the time comes, your training takes over.

When I first became a Christian, I ran people off. I was one of those annoying, hyperactive Christians that had to tell everybody, right away. But eventually I watched how some of my spiritual parents in CBMC shared their faith with others, and I learned more effective ways through the principles of lifestyle evangelism. I learned to talk about the truth without pushing people farther than they want to go. My focus changed from thinking about my need to share the gospel to thinking about the other person's need to hear the appropriate truth. I learned to look for common ground with an unsaved person, so that we had some point of connection. I also learned to be content with planting and watering, helping the unsaved person make small decisions rather than the big leap into the arms of the Lord.

One of the things that my mentors stressed with me was that I should think of some times when a biblical truth made an impact on me. Then I could talk about that truth without sounding like I was preaching. I don't mean only my testimony, but sharing with friends things I'd learned about business or marriage from the Bible. God has taught me so many lessons that it was easy to begin preparing a few stories that offered a window into my heart. I didn't want to be a spiritual porcupine, driving away the very people I wanted to win by sounding legalistic or preachy. Instead I simply wanted a method for being able to teach others what I know to be true.

By the way, a couple years ago CBMC created Living Proof, a video series that shows how Christians can learn to talk naturally about their Lord. It's being used by thousands of people around the world to train men and women how to effectively share their faith in their homes and offices. Living Proof is a powerful twelve-week group study, which includes a fifteen minute video session and a workbook. We've seen even the most timid people begin to reach out and share their faith stories.

I've found that if I can tell short, thirty-second stories about what I've learned or how I've seen God work, then I'll have opportunities to share them throughout my day. My stories are told as a natural part of the conversation, rather than gearing my conversation just toward dropping a spiritual bomb. And the stories create opportunities to establish my identity as a member of God's family, not as a member of some religious denomination. If the person I'm talking to isn't ready to hear more, that's fine with me. I've planted the seed, and now I'm going to allow God to cause the growth. My job is to continue building the relationship and seeking opportunities to lead the person one step closer to Christ.

One thing I've found necessary if you want to share truth with others is that you have to learn to *be* a testimony, not just *say* one. Know what God's Word says about moral standards, and let others see it in you without having to say it. Be aware of your personal walls—know what you can and cannot handle. It's okay to challenge your comfort zone, but stay within your personal boundaries. Develop a way to say no gracefully, so that you can tactfully reject a behavior that is not acceptable for you. Keep in mind that you can't please everyone. You have a responsibility to reach the lost, while at the same time you are called to not become a stumbling block to baby Christians. Learn to apply your own convictions gracefully, without alienating others. The rule of thumb is this: Determine God's perspective on moral and ethical issues, then act as a God-pleaser rather than a man-pleaser. In that way you'll set an example to everyone. Play to an audience of One, and you'll impact everyone for Him.

So, where are you involved with unbelievers now? In what area could you begin to include some unbelievers? You might find that lunches, sporting events, exercising, or even family trips offer a great opportunity for talking. Look for ways to serve the non-Christians in your life, and begin praying for their salvation. You might even be able to include another Christian or two in your activities, so that they can see your example and learn from you. One of the things I learned in the Marines is that we work best as a team, so take some of those people who are watching your example and teach them by doing the work of the ministry together.

Jewell Walker, a theater professor at the University of Wisconsin, has said, "Learning is a muscular thing. We learn by doing." If you really want to learn to teach others, start talking about your faith. Begin pulling others around you who also want to talk about their faith, and create a team with a common purpose of sharing the good news of Jesus Christ. Think about how Christ talked with people. He offered a loving, caring personality, met the needs of those around Him, spoke the truth bravely, and kept His mission of winning people clearly in mind. Whenever Christ interacted with people, whether it was His enemies or His disciples, the one issue that dominated the conversation was, "Who is Jesus?"

That's still the issue for most people, because the gospel is a person: Jesus Christ. Sometimes that gospel gets obscured. Christians will pick up a popular issue and make it part of the gospel message. For example, in recent years we've heard Christians who apparently want to preach the gospel of social justice, the gospel of prosperity, or the gospel of environmentalism, rather than the gospel of Jesus Christ. Others have preached a gospel of cultural rules, so that no one can possibly be a Christian unless he stops smoking, has short hair, or wears a white shirt and tie. That's not the gospel of Jesus Christ, that's a gospel of cultural interpretation. We don't have to preach a gospel of denominationalism or tradition. If we are going to be soldiers, sharing the truth with an unbelieving world, we need to follow the example of Paul, who said he would "become all things to all men so that by all means possible I might save some" (1 Corinthians 9:22).

I'm constantly amazed at the opportunities the Lord gives me to share my faith with my natural children and my spiritual children. One time, after Susy and I were coming back from a rather exhausting conference, a family was staying with us for the weekend. I felt totally drained. On top of that, our kids came down with the flu and began throwing up while our guests were sitting in the living room. That clogged the sink, so I was trying to talk to our friends while unclogging the drain in my bathroom. I wanted to call a plumber, but my friend was convinced we could fix it ourselves. We tried a plunger, then tried taking the trap apart. Nothing was working, so we eventually brought a hose in from outside and tried to force out the blockage. The pipes just backed up further.

So there I was, my clothes a mess, my bathroom torn apart, my kids sick, and I'm waiting for the plague of locusts to arrive and finish the job. But you know, God used that situation for good. My kids saw me submit to a plan of action from a friend who really wanted to help me. Teachers also need to be learners. They saw my faith come through in a crisis. It's amazing, but the Lord can even use disasters like that to teach the people around us.

Not that I always set such a good example. When Susanna, our youngest, was born, we had the worst snowstorm we'd seen in years. Twenty-four inches fell overnight, shutting down our city. All the power was out, so I warned our kids not to open the doors and let the heat out. We wanted to keep the newest little Downer warm. Not fifteen minutes later, I looked out and saw all the kids outside. I came marching down, barking at everyone. I wasn't going to listen to anyone; I just started telling everybody to get inside, then I read them the riot act for disobeying me. That's when my oldest daughter, Abigail, said to me, "Uh, Dad...the dogs were fighting. We went out to break them up, just like you told us to." Oops. I was wrong, and felt completely foolish. But the Lord used my mistake. I went to my kids and apologized for being angry and for shouting before I knew the facts. My daughter later told me she learned a lot about how a Christian makes up for his mistakes by watching me. So the Lord used me to teach her, even though I wasn't acting very maturely.

If you have children, you'll find you are always teaching them. Even when you don't realize it, they're watching and learning from you. I remember Susy calling me in tears one day, saying, "All I've done today is discipline and break up fights! I'm supposed to be home-schooling. There's no teaching going on today; it's all a waste!" But I asked her to think about the situation for a minute. True, she hadn't covered many history or math facts that day, but she had dealt with such important character issues as forgiveness, honesty, confession, and teamwork. Academics are important, but what do we need more in this country, strong spellers or people of strong character? "Susy," I told her, "you've been teaching all day without realizing it. You're doing a great job. Thanks for teaching our kids."

I try and take my children with me whenever I can in my ministry travels because I want them to see how a godly man lives. I see men who never have time to take their kids to a birthday party, but who always have time for golf, and I wonder if they realize what they're teaching. The people around you are watching your example, and if you have children they are watching with interest so that they can follow the pattern you set. You've probably noticed how children take on the characteristics of their parents. They laugh like their parents, think like their parents, and will learn the spiritual life from their parents. If church is something to be endured on Sunday but Christ never influences their parents' lives during the week, they'll soon learn that church isn't all that important.

Instead, they'll probably begin thinking that what's important is the acquisition of new things. *Parents* are responsible for the spiritual nurture of their children, not the Sunday School, the AWANA program, or the youth pastor. Are you setting an example of a soldier?

Christian men and women need to be teaching their children. Fathers need to take the time to teach their kids something of value. Mothers need to forget about investing in careers, which will never satisfy, and begin investing their whole lives in the kingdom. The BMW will rust, but the people in the kingdom will last forever.

I have a friend, an older woman, who teaches fifty women every week. Some are in one-on-one settings, some are in small groups, and she leads one large discussion group at her church. Every time I go to her house, she's on the phone, talking with somebody. I asked her one time who she was talking to, and she replied, "I'm discipling daughters, daughters-in-law, and young mothers." She talks with these women about husbands, sex, handling pressure, raising kids, handling money, dealing with anger, and managing their lives. She's a soldier who has become a teacher, helping prepare others to serve in the battle. Rather than watching television or joining social events, she's decided to spend her life as a discipler. She said to me one time, "I've seen many families turned around because of the mother," and she is determined to help those mothers become soldiers in the army of God.

The wife of a doctor, a friend in CBMC, began discipling a prostitute. They had nothing in common, but that young woman needed a mature Christian to teach her, and the doctor's wife knew that we all have been called to the commission of "making disciples." The changes in both people have been remarkable. That former prostitute is now on fire for the Lord, and her teacher is discipling more and more people to be soldiers for the King. If you can't talk about your faith, you won't lead anyone to Christ. If you can't teach about your faith, you won't help anyone become a soldier. You've got to be brave if you want to begin talking and teaching about your faith. You've got to become a strong soldier in Jesus Christ.

There is one more element to teaching that needs to be considered. A soldier who teaches others is also teachable himself. If you cannot learn from anyone else, you'll never be able to grow and change. In Numbers chapter thirteen there is a great story about being teachable. Moses, leading the nation of Israel through the wilderness, sends twelve men to spy out the Promised Land. He asks them to find out what the land is like, if it has good or bad soil, and if the towns are unwalled or fortified. The twelve went out, examined the land, then returned with their perspectives and samples of fruit that grew there. The people of Israel, who had just experienced the remarkable care and leadership of God, responded in a way that showed they were not teachable.

After the spies returned, they gathered the people together to say that the land flowed with milk and honey. But those good things were overshadowed by the bad. In Numbers 13:28, we read the words, "But the people who live there are powerful, and the cities are fortified and very large." Rather than focusing on the positive, the people of Israel focused on the negative. There was great potential in the Promised Land, but there was also a great problem. They had to choose on which they would focus. Teachable people choose to focus on the positive. For example, when Paul was in chains for preaching the gospel, he didn't complain about the chains; he praised God for the new opportunity to advance the gospel. Imagine having unbelievers chained to you all day—those Roman soldiers must have dreaded the thought of being chained to Paul! God never said being a Christian would be easy, but He does want us to look at the potential, not just the problem, to look at Him and not our circumstances.

The people of Israel went on to complain about all the tribes in Palestine that would have to be expelled. "We even saw descendants of Anak there. The Amalekites live in the Negev; the Hittites, Jebusites and Amorites live in the hill country; and the Canaanites live near the sea and along the Jordan....We can't attack those people; they are stronger than we are" (vv. 29,31). Notice how the people began to focus on fear. God had told them to possess the land. He had given it to them. But the Jews felt there had to be more to it. They thought they had to take it, not have it given to them.

Many people have that same trouble with salvation. They think there has to be more to it than the free gift of eternal life just by believing in Jesus. So they reject the basic plan of God. That's what the Jews did in Numbers chapter thirteen. The more they talked about their fear, the greater the problem became. Fear even distorted their perception of the problem, so that pretty soon they were saying, "The land we explored devours those living in it. All the people we saw there are of great size...we seemed like grasshoppers in our own eyes" (vv. 32, 33). Rather than being willing to accept the teaching of God, they focused on fear. Pretty soon their fear was over-coming their good judgment.

The next problem they had was in focusing on themselves rather than God. "If only we had died in Egypt!" they began to mutter. "Why is the Lord bringing us to this land only to let us fall by the sword...wouldn't it be better for us to go back to Egypt?" (Numbers 14:2,3). After all the miraculous escapes the Lord had provided, His people had already decided they were going to lose. Rather than looking at God's mighty power, or His bountiful provision, they looked at themselves.

Any time you take your eyes off the Lord in battle, you suffer. When Peter was walking on the water, he did fine as long as his eyes remained on Jesus. But when he began to look at the wind and waves, he became afraid and started to sink.

All he had to do was look to Jesus and he would be safe. Keeping our eyes focused on the Lord allows Him to teach us.

One time, when the Jews began grumbling against God, the Lord sent poisonous snakes into the camp as punishment. When they repented of their sins, God did not take the poisonous snakes away; instead He had Moses raise a bronze snake on a pole in the center of the camp. All anyone had to do when he was bitten was turn and look at the bronze snake, and he would be saved. It was God's way of saying, "Keep you eyes on Me and My salvation." And the funny thing is, I'll bet some people refused to look at that snake. Some of them probably figured they had a better plan for solving their snake bite. Or maybe they just didn't believe in the healing power of that bronze serpent. So when they were bitten, they died, refusing the lesson of the Lord.

Good soldiers are teachable. They focus on the potential, not the problem. They focus on the Lord rather than on themselves or their fears. They willingly listen to the teaching of the Lord and allow Him to change them.

It got worse for Israel. Numbers chapter fourteen also reveals how they rejected God's leadership: "We should choose a leader and go back to Egypt" (v. 4). Moses was God's man, as the Lord had clearly shown on several occasions, but the people were willing to throw it all away. Their best solution was to return to Egypt, where they had been mistreated slaves. And not only did they reject God's leadership, they also forgot His faithfulness. When faced with a problem, the miracles of manna in the desert, water from the rock, and the parting of the Red Sea were all forgotten.

Like Judas Iscariot would do centuries later, the people of Israel spent time with the Lord and still rejected Him. Their willingness to reject His leadership and forget His faithfulness allowed them to incite His anger. God was utterly disappointed in His people. Whenever we limit our vision to ourselves and our world, we force God out of our lives. You see, while we have a tendency to forget about the Lord, He never forgets about us. When we want to focus on the problem, God is focused on the big picture. Think about the reason Israel was in the wilderness to begin with—God was calling them to become totally dependent upon Him.

Sometimes we miss God's teaching because our focus is in the wrong place. For example, had we been at the side of Jesus, we no doubt would have thought that His dying was a big mistake. But Christ dying on the cross turned out to be the key to peace with God for all people. It was a hard experience, but it turned out for our best. When Paul suffered for preaching the gospel, he had to keep in mind that the problems he faced were overshadowed by the big picture: The gospel was moving out into the world. God can work through us if we allow Him to.

God has a plan for your life, and the power to accomplish it. He needs to be able to change your life and teach you if He is going to use you to teach others. Part of being a good teacher is to be teachable. One year I was discipling a young doctor who was at the top of his field, but suffering from anxiety attacks. He needed to learn from me, but I needed some access to his life, so I invited him to teach me about gardening, which was his hobby. Through this he saw that I was teachable, and that made him willing to listen to me when it was my turn to teach.

One day, as he was complaining about his lack of peace, I suggested taking a look at what God had to say about his problem. I opened up my Bible to Romans chapter five and read these words: "Therefore, since we have been justified through faith, we have peace with God through our Lord Jesus Christ, through whom we have gained access by faith into this grace in which we now stand. And we rejoice in the hope of the glory of God. Not only so, but we also rejoice in our sufferings, because we know that suffering produces perseverance; perseverance, character; and character, hope. And hope does not disappoint us, because God has poured out his love into our hearts by the Holy Spirit, whom he had given us" (Romans 5:1-5).

After reading through that passage and talking about what it meant, he looked at me and said, "I don't have peace. I never have had it. I don't think I'm a Christian."

"I don't think so, either," I told him. So he accepted Christ, and found freedom from his anxiety. I would never have had a chance to teach him if I had not first allowed him to teach me.

Soldiers can teach others. They know how to share their faith, how to explain it to others, and how to prepare other Christians for fighting in the spiritual war. They also keep their eyes on the Lord, allowing Him to teach them and change them so that they can become better soldiers. More than anything else, that's what I want for my life. I want the Lord to be teaching me, shaping me into a more mature soldier, so that I can better lead other people to maturity in Him.

CHAPTER THIRTEEN

No
Rest
for the
Weary

The army of God will be no more successful than its soldiers. If there are strong, brave soldiers, the army will do well in the spiritual war. If it has fearful, weak soldiers, it will fail to impact the battle significantly. The key to doing well is to train good soldiers, and that's part of my calling at Christian Business Men's Committee. I want to help train an army of men who love God and are dedicated to His cause in this world.

Paul once wrote to his young friend Timothy, a timid man facing persecution, and encouraged him to remember that nothing comes easy. Anybody who is going to make an impact on the world for Jesus Christ is going to have to work hard. There's no rest in this war. If you're going to lead others into battle, you'll have to bravely set an example of hard work. Every successful Christian leader I know works hard. None of them has found a way to be successful in battle by taking it easy.

In 2 Timothy chapter two, Paul offers eight different pictures of leadership that describe the lives of those who would serve God. A quick study of those leadership pictures will help you to understand the importance of working hard if you want to get anything accomplished.

Teacher

"You therefore, my son, be strong in the grace that is in Christ Jesus. And the things which you have heard from me in the presence of many witnesses, these entrust to faithful men, who will be able to teach others also" (2 Timothy 2:1-2). As we've already seen, everybody who wants to change their world for the cause of Christ will have to be a teacher. That verse is particularly interesting because of the importance it places on producing teachers. There are four generations at work in those verses. Paul (generation one) is teaching Timothy (generation two) about entrusting the truth to reliable men (generation three) who will be able to teach others (generation four).

I was sitting at my desk, perturbed over a seemingly impossible legal problem, when I got a call from Steven, a man I had led to the Lord and discipled about ten years earlier. He barely said hello before blurting out, "Congratulations, Phil, you're a great-grandfather!" I was so immersed in the cares of the world that I didn't have the foggiest notion what he was talking about. Hearing my silence, he asked me, "Phil, did you hear what I said? You're a great-grandfather." Then it hit me: Steven, one of my "Timothies," had led a man to the Lord, and that guy had just led someone else to the Savior.

"Really?" I replied. "That's great, Steven. When can I meet him?" New birth always takes precedence over the routine of our daily lives. To tell the truth, I can't tell you much about the legal problem I was struggling with that day, but I rejoice in the eternal soul that God has reproduced out of my life. My goal is to be a fourth-generation reproducer, because that was the goal of my spiritual father, grandfather, great-grandfather, and great-great-grandfather.

The church has to seek to produce reproducers. There can be no compromise on this; the man of God must be a student of the Bible, able to articulate its truth and pass it along to the next generation. Without "next generation thinking," the army of God will die out.

Soldier

"Endure hardship with us like a good soldier of Christ Jesus. No one serving as a soldier gets involved in civilian affairs—he wants to please his commanding officer" (vv. 3-4). If you're going to be effective for the Lord in this world, you're going to have to be willing to suffer the hardships that come with the role. The fact is, it's tough to be a Christian in our world today. We're in a war, and people get wounded in wars. There is deep hurt and deep grieving for those involved in the battle. But the battle goes on, and we must choose to fight or be destroyed.

One of the things I learned in Viet Nam is that there are no part-time soldiers. You can't take a day off when you're on the front lines. That's when you get killed.

JoJo was an excellent Marine machine gunner, but he had one life-threatening weakness: He could not bring himself to urinate in front of the other guys in the squad. Here we were, a highly trained and effective fighting unit, laying down our lives for one another deep in enemy territory, and JoJo would wander off the trail that had been secured by the point man so that he could walk into the undergrowth and relieve himself. In doing so, he not only risked his own life, but the life of every one of us in the platoon. Our outfit not only operated in North Vietnamese army territory, but in an area known for having many booby-traps. The enemy would lay mines, made of artillery or unexploded aircraft shells, with small trip wires running through the thicket. Once an area was cleared, you never varied from the path, especially for something as mundane as JoJo's particular mission.

As hard as I tried as the squad leader, I could never break JoJo of the habit. One day he hit a "bouncing Betty" mine, a spring trigger which launches an explosive about head high. It blew JoJo's head clean off. He had just wanted to take a few minutes away from the front lines, but it cost him his life.

It takes total commitment to be a soldier, and Paul says the only concern for a soldier is pleasing his commander. You've got to learn to trust and obey what Jesus says, even when you disagree with it or don't like it. As our Commanding Officer, He knows more than we do. He's got a strategy for winning.

If we're going to be soldiers, we can't place ourselves in situations where our families or ministries are left unarmed in a dangerous area. Sam was a very disciplined man, who threw himself into Bible study, memory work, and exercise every morning. However he joined a new health club which had female training assistants, and he couldn't handle the pressure. Rather than leaving the area, he chose to stay, and ended up having a sexual encounter with one of the female trainers.

As he sat at my desk, crying, he asked, "Do I have to tell my wife? What will I say to our kids? And what about the guys I'm discipling?" Then, looking at the floor, he muttered, "Oh, God, why'd I do it?" Like JoJo, Sam left the battle. He isn't dead, but he's a serious casualty in the war.

There are no part-time soldiers. Use your life to please

Him. It will be difficult, but He has called you to fight. Be willing to suffer for the cause.

Athlete

"Similarly, if anyone competes as an athlete, he does not receive the victor's crown unless he competes according to the rules" (2 Timothy 2:5). A sprinter has very specific rules to follow: Stay frozen in your blocks at the ready, don't start until you hear the gun, and stay in your lane throughout the race. If he breaks the rules, he'll be disqualified. How fast he runs won't matter; his rule violation will end his chance to compete. It takes a commitment to excellence for an athlete to succeed. If you're going to accomplish anything for God in this world, you're going to have to have that same sort of dedicated integrity.

Dedication is often more important than natural ability. I remember being impressed with the great basketball player Larry Bird's work ethic. During a television interview just after his Boston Celtics had won another championship, Bird was asked by a reporter what his plans were for the off-season. "I'll take two weeks off, then start practicing my shooting," he said in a very matter-of-fact way. I knew that everybody else on his team planned to take a long summer break, but not Larry Bird. The reason he got to be the best was because of his willingness to work hard at the things he needed for success. He wanted to win, and he wanted to play by the rules, so he simply worked harder than anybody else to get better.

Sal is a good friend. A committed Christian, he was elected to Congress, well on his way to becoming one of the favorites of the statewide political scene. He had a great education, impeccable business career, a beautiful family, and a strong faith in Christ. He was the perfect leader, and many thought of him as a future Senator for his state. The problem was that Sal insisted doing things his way. When it came time for an important contract, his former business associate was a natural for the job. To keep the project on schedule, Sal carefully designed a method to get his friend the contract rather than arranging competitive bids. When a political enemy produced a tape recording that suggested Sal had done an end run on the proper procedure, Sal lost his integrity in the eyes of the electorate. He left office in disgrace.

A soldier who loses his integrity can never be trusted. I once woke up in the jungle to find our lookout asleep on the job. That sort of laziness could have cost me my life. He was an undisciplined man, and soon no one wanted to team with him. Soldiers unwilling to be dedicated often ended the war dead. If you wanted to survive, you learned the rules of survival and you adhered to them.

Maintaining your integrity is crucial. I've seen far too many guys lose their integrity in the spiritual war and be disqualified from any further ministry. Sexual sin, greed, and pride have forced a lot of people out of God's army. The apostle Paul once said, "I do not run like a man running aimlessly; I do not fight like a man beating the air. No, I beat my body and make it my slave so that after I have preached to others, I myself will not be disqualified for the prize" (1 Corinthians 9:26-27). If you're going to be an effective soldier, you need to maintain your integrity, just as an athlete does in order to complete the race.

Farmer

"The hardworking farmer should be the first to receive a share of the crops. Reflect on what I am saying, for the Lord will give you insight into all this" (2 Timothy 2:6-7). Being a soldier is heavy labor, just like being a farmer. There are few breaks and few vacations. When we were in the field as soldiers, there was never a time we were "off-duty." As long as we were on the front lines, we were ready to fight. An infantryman learns to catch a few hours of sleep at a time, because there aren't any eight-hour breaks. This is war, which calls for a special kind of commitment to your job. Sometimes you labor until exhaustion. But one thing I found to be true: If you work hard, you get results.

Branch Rickey, the genius behind the great years of the Brooklyn and Los Angeles Dodgers, once said, "Luck is the residue of design. It seems the harder I work, the luckier I get." Success doesn't usually come by dumb luck; it comes by hard work. That's something every farmer knows. If you want to have a big crop in the fall, you've got to work hard planting in the spring. Crops don't grow themselves. One of the truths of Scripture is that at the end of our lives, everybody will get what they deserve. The unsaved will be judged according to their sin, and God won't be arbitrary or unfair in the least. The saved will be forgiven their sins, but will be judged for their works, and God will reward based on that service. Everybody will earn what they get; there will be no fooling God.

After being spiritually birthed by a doctor and our marriage restored, Susy and I decided to go to him for a different kind of baby delivery—our natural children. We were asking the Lord to start our family, and Jim became her obstetrician and gynecologist. I won't embarrass Jim by telling his age; suffice it to say that most doctors his age are relaxing on a beach somewhere. But Jim continues to see patients, handle emergencies, and deliver physical babies during the day, while birthing spiritual children in his off hours. He birthed a total of seven Downers—our six natural children, and their father, who some would say is the biggest baby of all!

His busy schedule would do most men in, but on top of his medical appointments, deliveries, and rounds, Jim is meeting with four to six men every week, continuing his investment in kingdom returns. His goal is not just to be a deliverer of physical babies on earth, but a deliverer of spiritual children into God's eternal kingdom. The fruit from his life, and that of his wife, impacts the world more greatly every day.

I have always appreciated Paul's words to the church at Thessalonica, where he commends them for their hard work: "We always thank God for all of you, mentioning you in our prayers. We continually remember your work produced by faith, your labor prompted by love, and your endurance inspired by hope in our Lord Jesus Christ" (1 Thessalonians 1:2-3). In that passage Paul uses three words for "work," each more intense than the previous. First he commends the Thessalonians for their work, and the word he uses refers to activity. Apparently the believers in Thessalonica were busy for the Lord. Second, he commends them for their labor, and that Greek work refers to hard physical toil. In other words, those Christians weren't just busy, they were busy at something that was very tough work. Third, he commends them for their endurance, a word that refers to doing work for a long period of time. So the Thessalonian believers were doing hard work for extended time, obeying the Lord in His calling. And the motivation behind their work? Faith in God, love for God, and hope in God.

The reason God's soldiers will work hard for His cause today is not just out of an obligation, but out of our love for and faith in the Lord. We're called to work hard, but we know God loves us, has forgiven our sin, and is right now preparing a place for our eternity. Like farmers awaiting the harvest, we work hard now in expectation of our future reward.

Prisoner

"Remember Jesus Christ, raised from the dead, descended from David. This is my gospel, for which I am suffering even to the point of being chained like a criminal. But God's Word is not chained. Therefore I endure everything for the sake of the elect, that they too may obtain the salvation that is in Christ Jesus, with eternal glory" (2 Timothy 2:8-10). Many of the early Christians knew what it was like to suffer hardship for the cause of Christ. Stephen was stoned by Jews in Jerusalem. Paul was eventually beheaded. Andrew was crucified on an X-shaped cross in Edessa, continuing to preach the gospel from the cross for two days before expiring. Peter was crucified on an upside-down cross, not believing himself worthy to die on a cross in the same manner as the Lord Jesus. James, Philip, Matthew, Mark, Jude, Bartholomew, and Thomas also suffered martyrdom for the Lord's sake. They died as soldiers in the battle, their lives taken for preaching the truth to people who chose to believe lies.

Jesus had promised that following Him would be a hard path. He began His ministry by calling for His people to love their enemies and to do good to their persecutors, something that runs contrary to human nature. When another teacher came to Him and promised to follow the Lord, Jesus replied, "Foxes have holes and birds of the air have nests, but the Son of Man has no place to lay his head" (Matthew 8:20). He told His followers that they would be like sheep among wolves, and that a life with God would be difficult. "Whoever acknowledges me before men, I will also acknowledge him before my Father in heaven. But whoever disowns me before men, I will disown him before my Father in heaven. Do not suppose that I have come to bring peace to the earth. I did not come to bring peace, but a sword. For I have come to turn a man against his father, a daughter against her mother, a daughter-in-law against her mother-in-law—a man's enemies will be the member of his own household. Anyone who loves his father or mother more than me is not worthy of me; anyone who loves his son or daughter more than me is not worthy of me; and anyone who does not take his cross and follow me is not worthy of me. Whoever finds his life will lose it, and whoever loses his life for my sake will find it" (Matthew 10:34-39).

That's a hard teaching, but then Jesus was in the business of sharing hard things. Our world has tended to emphasize Christ's forgiveness and mercy, while ignoring His holiness and justice. God is a jealous God, and He demands to be loved above all else. The person who truly loves God is bound to suffer, because he lives in a world that hates God. Christians have suffered as martyrs and objects of ridicule since the time of Christ's arrest. "As servants of God we commend ourselves in every way," Paul wrote to the Corinthians. "In great endurance, in troubles, hardships, and distresses; in beatings, imprisonments, and riots; in hard work, sleepless nights and hunger; in purity, understanding, patience and kindness; in the Holy Spirit and in sincere love; in truthful speech and in the power of God; with weapons of righteousness in the right hand and in the left; through glory and dishonor, bad report and good report; genuine, yet regarded as impostors; known, yet regarded as unknown; dying, and yet we live on; beaten, and yet not killed; sorrowful, yet always rejoicing; poor, yet making many rich; having nothing, and yet possessing everything" (2 Corinthians 6:3-10). The apostle understood that being a soldier meant becoming a prisoner for the cause of Christ.

Prisoners don't get any breaks. There isn't an afternoon when they get to take an hour off from being a prisoner. They are locked up or punished for their actions, just as soldiers in the army of God are punished by the world for not conforming to its pattern. The writer to the Hebrews said that some Christians "were tortured and refused to be released, so that they might gain a better resurrection. Some faced jeers and flogging, while still others were chained and put in prison. They were stoned; they were sawed in two; they were put to death by the sword. They went about in sheepskins and goatskins, destitute, persecuted, and mistreated—the world was not worthy of them. They wandered in deserts and mountains, and in caves and holes in the ground" (Hebrews 11:35-38).

Christians used to know what it was like to suffer. I worry about Christians in our own day who have never faced persecution. A church under persecution is pure, since only the true believers dare to participate. But it has been easy to be a Christian in our culture, and I think many have forgotten how to fight. They have never been taught that we are in a war; in fact, the concept of warfare is foreign to them. When persecution increases on Christians in our modern world, as it surely will, only the soldiers will know how to remain strong.

After the fall of the Iron Curtain, many stories about the bravery and hard work of Christians under communism finally made their way to the West. One story was that of a small Baptist church which met in Moscow. Under relentless persecution from government authorities, one Sunday evening the doors burst open and two soldiers with machine guns came walking down the center aisle. "Anyone not willing to die for their faith had better leave," growled the armed men, and much of the flock scattered out the doors. Only a faithful few remained, huddled at the altar, as those two soldiers shut and bolted the church doors, moved to the front of the church, and whispered, "We're Christians too. We just wanted to know whom we could trust."

Christians will suffer for their hard work in this world. It will require men of bravery to take a stand for God in a world that rejects Him. But all we must do is take a look at the men and women of Christendom who have suffered and been imprisoned for the Name. History is replete with the names of Christians who have become prisoners for Christ's sake. John Bunyan, author of *Pilgrim's Progress*, spent twelve years in jail for his faith. William Penn, founder of the state of Pennsylvania, was severely persecuted for his faith. William Tyndale, John Huss, and Thomas Cramner are just a few of the more famous names who have been martyred for the Lord, though the list is much longer.

George, the president of the Chamber of Commerce for his city, was one of the main movers behind the redevelopment of his city's downtown business district. He worked to get ten Fortune 500 corporate headquarters relocated to his city, and for ten years was the prime mover in getting several other economic infusions that regenerated the downtown and moved his city to the top of the U.S. economic scale. A Christian, he had continued discipling men and sharing Christ through evangelistic outreach meetings in the central business district. Every year he put together a mayor's prayer breakfast that drew a thousand men, and year after year a large percentage of people made a commitment to Jesus Christ, were followed up by teams of Christians, and led into discipling relationships.

One year, as I sat at my table enjoying the breakfast, I wondered how the local bank president could once again sit through hearing the great testimonies of Christians and not receive Jesus Christ as his Savior. We'd been praying for that bank president for years, and on this day he looked particularly uncomfortable and bolted from the meeting. Nine months later, when that man took over as president of the Chamber of Commerce, to the shock of everyone, he fired George.

At the pinnacle of his career, George was dumped simply for being a Christian. There is no doubt in anyone's mind that he was being persecuted for his faith by someone who refused Christ's gospel and decided to take it out on the messenger. Times are coming when this sort of conduct will be considered mild, and we'd better be ready for it as soldiers.

Becoming a soldier is a sacrifice. You sacrifice your will and your way to follow the will of God. Paul, in describing his own experiences, once said, "I have worked harder, been in prison more frequently, been flogged more severely, and been exposed to death again and again. Five times I received from the Jews the forty lashes minus one. Three times I was beaten with rods, once I was stoned, three times I was shipwrecked, I spent a night and a day in the open sea, I have been constantly on the move. I have been in danger from rivers, in danger from bandits, in danger from my own countrymen, in danger from Gentiles; in danger in the city, in danger in the country, in danger at sea; and in danger from false brothers. I have labored and toiled and have often gone without sleep; I have known hunger and thirst and have often gone without food; I have been cold and naked. Besides everything else, I face daily the pressure of my concern for all the churches. Who is weak, and I do not feel weak? Who is led into sin, and I do not inwardly burn?" (2 Corinthians 11:23-29). Yet Paul concludes that passage by saying, "If I must boast, I will boast of the things that show my weakness....He said to me, 'My grace is sufficient for you, for my power is made perfect in weakness.' Therefore I will boast all the more gladly about my weaknesses, so that Christ's power may rest on me. That is why, for Christ's sake, I delight in weaknesses, in insults, in hardships, in persecutions, in difficulties. For when I am weak, then I am strong" (2 Corinthians 11:30, 12:9-10).

God's divine power is best displayed against the backdrop of human weakness, so that He alone is praised. Rather than do away with suffering, God gives us the grace to endure it. That grace transforms our perspective on being a prisoner for Christ. Those experiences which we would not normally desire are welcomed because God's power can be so clearly seen in them. His strength is evidenced through my weakness.

Workman

"Keep reminding them of these things. Warn them before God against quarreling about words; it is of no value, and only ruins those who listen. Do your best to show yourself as one approved, a workman who does not need to be ashamed and who correctly handles the word of truth. Avoid godless chatter, because those who indulge in it will become more and more ungodly" (2 Timothy 2:14-16). A workman does his job; he doesn't spend all day flapping his jaw about unimportant things. As soldiers, we aren't to spend our time arguing about every little detail. We are simply to obey our Commanding Officer. Work to please Him and you'll find yourself becoming much more effective in the battle.

Give yourself to excellence. You've probably played golf or tennis with somebody who talked a great game. He made himself sound like the return of Jack Nicklaus, or the spitting image of Bjorn Borg. But then you began to play, and you found his hands to be not nearly as good as his mouth. As Paul tells Timothy, don't spend your time blabbing about the war. *Fight* the war.

Vessel

"In a large house there are articles not only of gold and silver, but also of wood and clay; some are for noble purposes and some for ignoble. If a man cleanses himself from the latter, he will be an instrument for noble purposes, made holy, useful to the Master and prepared to do any good work" (2 Timothy 2:20-21). All vessels do the same thing: They hold things. Some are fancy and some are plain, but they all do the same type of work. Yet some have been set aside for noble purposes. Perhaps they hold the King's crown, or are a receptacle for the King's wine. Paul tells Timothy that a Christian soldier needs to set himself apart from ignoble vessels. Become a pure vessel, set apart for the Lord's work, and useful to the Master. Make yourself ready to be used by God, available at all times.

When I first became a Christian, I was not a useful vessel for the Savior. My language was bad, my attitude needed to be changed, and the way I treated people kept God from using me in any significant way in the lives of others. So God had to change me. If I was going to be a vessel that was ready and available to work on His behalf, I would have to set myself apart. So I watched the power of God work in my life, and I've seen Him begin to use me as His implement in this world. As a clean vessel, I've been used to help introduce others into the kingdom, and assist them in their growth toward Christlikeness. I could never have done that when I was an ignoble vessel.

Jesus used Matthew the tax-collector, the lowliest person in Jewish society, to write the gospel directed at Jewish readers. Matthew's gospel describes Jesus as the anointed one, the Messiah for whom the Jews had been waiting. It was inconceivable that a tax-collector would be the one to instruct the Jewish religious leaders on the Messiah, yet the Lord used Matthew as His instrument for propagating the gospel. Christ used John, who had been one of the "sons of thunder," to write about the love of God. John wasn't a loving guy at the start of Christ's ministry. He was a loud and profane man, who once asked Jesus if He wanted to send fire from heaven down to destroy somebody who was heckling the Lord. Yet John's life changed, and he was the one who told us that "God is love." It almost seems as if Jesus deliberately picked guys who were considered losers and outcasts to be close to him. Yet the Lord set an example in His life, moving the twelve toward maturity, so that He could use them for His purposes.

Being a Christian soldier is hard work, and the Lord has to shape and mold you so that you perform the perfect function He has planned for you. Set yourself apart in purity and godliness, make yourself constantly available for His use, and you will begin to see the Lord use you in mighty ways.

Servant

"And the Lord's servant must not quarrel; instead, he must be kind to everyone, able to teach, not resentful. Those who oppose him he must gently instruct, in hope that God will grant them repentance leading them to a knowledge of the truth, and that they will come to their senses and escape from the trap of the devil, who had taken them captive to do his will" (2 Timothy 2:24). The last picture of a mature man of God that Paul offers to Timothy is that of a servant, which we'll be looking at more in depth later. Note that, as a soldier, you are God's servant, not man's. You are to do God's will, not the will of the people around you.

Everybody is a slave to someone. Christians are slaves to God, non-Christians are slaves to the world. God's servant is marked by gentleness, a willingness to listen, and a habit of kindness. Paul warns Timothy not to argue when opposed, for no one has ever won a convert by winning an argument. Instead we are to be humble and gentle, submissive to God and showing a sweet spirit to others. If you set that sort of an example to the Christians around you, you'll soon find that you've got a team of positive soldiers with whom you can serve.

One day, more than a decade ago, I sat in my brother-in-law Tom's car, hardly believing that his fiancé Anita was dead. Anita had been struck down by a minister who was on his way to church. Tom was going to have to wear the suit he'd bought for his wedding to his fiancé's funeral. I simply didn't know what to say. Instead of saying nothing, I started with Romans 8:28, moved through Psalm 37 and was just getting to 1 Thessalonians 5:16-17 when Tom spoke. "You know, Phil, sometimes it's good just to listen."

He's right. Sometimes a servant needs to close his mouth and allow the Holy Spirit to work. When you put the gentleness of the Lord to work, you often have a wonderful opportunity to minister.

That's the biblical picture of a hard-working soldier for Christ. He is a teacher of others; as devoted as a world-class athlete; as patient and nurturing as a farmer; willing to suffer as a prisoner for Christ; doing his work diligently like a good workman; a pure and available vessel in God's hands; and a servant to the Lord, treating others with gentleness and kindness since that is the example Christ set for us all. God's standards are high, but if we follow His example, we can be greatly used for His cause.

Able to Handle God's Word

E very morning at 4:00 a.m. my alarm clock rings—actually three alarm clocks ring, because it takes a lot to get me out of bed—and I stumble my way to the dining-room table. It's hard for me to get up that early, but it's necessary. I have to spend time in the Word, allowing the Lord to cleanse me and prepare me for another day of battle. I lay myself open every day, and God makes me clean.

After a soldier has gone through a battle, the first thing he does is clean his weapon. When you use a gun it collects grime, and since your life depends upon your weapon, you don't want it to jam or get rusty. So you regularly tear it apart and clean it, to make sure it is prepared for the next firefight. I take the same approach to my spiritual life. It gets put into a battle each day, so I want to make sure my life is clean and ready to go before I head back to the war. When I first started my Christian walk, I found myself getting worn down by the daily grind. I went to a man for whom I had great respect and asked, "How do you keep going?" I'll never forget his reply: "If I don't get something from the Word every day, I'm dead." From that point on, I've made it a priority to begin each day in prayer and Bible study. As a soldier setting an example to others, I figure I have to feed myself spiritually each day and be able to train others to do so, or I'm not doing my job.

This is no secret. *You need a daily quiet time*. You will never be an effective soldier without daily time in the Word. You will never grow into maturity without a personal time alone with God. You can hear great sermons in church or on the radio, but those who grow spiritually are the ones who feed themselves. Nothing has made a greater impact on my life than spending time with God each morning. I have had men I've discipled contact me and say, "My life changed when you taught me how to have a daily quiet time." We've all assented to the importance of quiet time intellectually, but most of us haven't invested in it because we didn't have the discipline or we didn't believe it would make that much of a difference. But I'm here to testify that my quiet time has significantly influenced my life and the lives around me, and I've seen that same story multiplied time after time in the lives of the men I've discipled—and in those who have discipled me.

The goal of every soldier should be to develop a one-on-one time each day that offers a vibrant encounter with the Maker of the universe. In your time with God you'll find that He'll offer you guidance, bring you strength, and overwhelm your troubles and concerns with peace. Eventually you'll begin to think from God's perspective; the Lord will dominate your goals and dreams. When you sit down to meditate on the

Lord each morning, don't leave until His thoughts are your thoughts. Then you can let God use you as His implement in this world. My quiet time refreshes me, gives me a new attitude, and allows me to carry my responsibilities to my job and my family with a sense of confidence and assurance.

Do you remember how you felt when you first became a Christian? You may have experienced an unsurpassable joy, knowing that God loved you. You probably experienced true peace, confident that your sins were forgiven. You had an excitement that made you want to burst out and tell others about your faith. You were willing to surrender everything to Jesus Christ. But perhaps you no longer feel that way. Now your spiritual life is drudgery, or it's just not a peak experience for you. If that describes your spiritual walk, I'll bet you're not having a daily quiet time. You have to spend time with the Lord each day until you experience what you did on that day you first met the Lord Jesus Christ. If you want to find a fruitful, spirit-filled life, you've got to spend as much time as necessary to be clean before the Lord. You can complain that you don't have time for daily devotions, but you'll never grow into maturity until you make the time.

For me, that has meant getting up early every morning, something I hate to do. I'm a night person, and I enjoy taking my time waking up and getting going each morning. But I can't allow myself that luxury if the Lord is going to prepare me for my day. I'm a soldier, and I get up early to get ready for battle. You don't prepare for a battle by getting everything ready at bedtime. You can't focus on Christ while you're sleeping! Get up in the morning and begin your day by focusing on the Lord.

You can start simply. Plan to spend seven to ten minutes each morning, and grow from there. Simply get up fifteen minutes earlier than normal, read one chapter in your Bible, spend a few minutes praying about the greatest needs in your life, and ask the Lord to help you in your day. If you do that, you'll find several things start to happen. First, you'll begin to approach your day from a new perspective. You'll be thinking about the principles of God and how you can apply them to your day. Second, the Lord will begin to speak to you, and you'll find yourself becoming more mature in your faith. Third, you'll start to have some solid examples of answered prayer.

As you grow in your daily quiet time, each of these elements will remain the same, but you'll probably spend more time at them. You can begin reading more Scripture, perhaps both an Old and New Testament chapter. As I said earlier, many men read five Psalms and one Proverb each day, others prefer reading several chapters from one book. If you use *The Daily Walk*, you'll find yourself reading through the entire Bible in one year. The issue isn't so much the quantity of reading, but that you are reading a significant portion of God's Word on a daily basis. That gives you an adequate supply of spiritual food, so that you don't face your day undernourished. It's hard to fight when you're weak from hunger, so don't be afraid to gorge yourself on the Word.

Your prayer time will increase as you begin to see the Lord answer your prayers. You may want to start a list, so that you've got some things you pray for each day, or on particular days. For example, some people take one day just to praise the Lord; others will have one day set aside just to pray for the salvation of friends. You can take time for praising and thanksgiving, prayers of confession, or prayers of adoring the Lord. There is no "right" pattern for praying. Prayer is simply having a conversation with God. You can ask Him to help you change those areas of your life that need the Spirit's help. You can pray that He will help you to love others. I have a list of people for whom I pray for God's blessing, and another list of those whom I want to see come to Christ. I make sure those names get prayed for each week.

Of course, you can also keep a list of things you would like God to do for yourself or others, and you can keep track of that list so that you create a monument to the work of God in your life. If you are struggling with decisions, ask God to make His will clear to you. Remind yourself to pray that you will accept God's will, and pray that He'll be glorified in your life. It's good to occasionally wrestle in prayer over issues. Spend as much time as you need to feel you've gained the mind of the Lord. In our hurry-up world, we've lost the nature of wrestling in prayer. It can only be regained by those willing to spend time alone with the Lord.

There is something else in your quiet time; something that often gets overlooked. In addition to Bible reading and prayer, every man should spend time in meditation and study. Many Christians seem to fear the entire topic of meditation, thinking it linked to eastern religions, but Scripture is replete with commands for God's people to meditate on His Word. Meditation isn't a strange or ethereal concept; it is simply allowing your mind to ponder the thoughts of God. When you meditate on Scripture, you simply read a short passage, then close your eyes and think about what it says. I'll often pray this prayer: "Lord, allow my thoughts to recede, and You fill my mind with Your thoughts."

I use the practice of outlining my Bible, which slows me down and allows the Word to soak into my life through meditation. If you want to go to the next level in your daily quiet time, spend two mornings a week meditating on passages of Scripture.

The other discipline to master is that of studying the Bible. That's when you take a book and analyze it. First you read it through several times, to familiarize yourself with it. When I wanted to come to a better understanding of 1 John, I read it through every day for a month. After one week it seemed to get old, as though I knew it completely. But during the third week new things started to emerge from my reading. I felt that I was finally tapping into the message God has for us in that important book.

Try and grasp the overall message of the book, then explore the historical background. Who wrote it? When? Why? What was the occasion that prompted this book? After that you can begin to outline the book, then cross-reference the verses to other parts of Scripture. Give each chapter a title, and start to create a flow chart that pictorially describes the events or the message in the book. Next you can chart each chapter, noting the divisions, the interpretations, and the application in each section. You can pull out key words and phrases for further study, or explore problem passages by cross-referencing to other passages. Then you can explore the message and progression of each paragraph, and even look at the grammar, facts, and application of each verse. Remember, these are the very words of God. The Holy Spirit spoke through the various biblical authors to select the right word for each verse. The words of God are perfect and complete, and their message can change lives. You can use any version with which you're comfortable, but I'm using the New American Standard Version of the *International Inductive Study Bible*, from Kay Arthur's Precepts Ministries, and I've found it to be particularly helpful.

The other sort of study is a topical study, wherein you select a topic of interest, build a list of Bible references relating to it, then organize the facts in those verses into some sort of coherent outline. Expect the Bible to teach you vital truths. Look for it to offer wisdom and insight into your life and your relationships. God wants to meet you each day and change your life through that meeting. Jeremiah 33:3 says, "Call to me and I will answer you and tell you great and unsearchable things you do not know." The great God of creation wants to speak to you. Can you say you aren't interested?

If you can't seem to force yourself to get up in the morning, have a partner call you and get you up. If you just can't get into Bible study, offer to teach a Sunday School class so that you have to study your Bible each week. Sure, it's a crutch, but remember that crutches serve a useful purpose. They help us get by while something is broken. If your quiet time is broken, use something as a crutch for a while to help you survive, then slowly learn to walk on your own again.

Perhaps the greatest practice that has changed my life has been Bible memory. The Lord calls us to renew our minds, so that we will not be conformed to this world. Committing to memory passages of Scripture helps me to maintain God's perspective on my life.

I'm not legalistic about my quiet time. There are days where it's impossible for me to spend my normal time with God, so I don't. My quiet time isn't designed for me to earn God's favor, but for me to learn God's thoughts. I see it as a valuable time for getting my life together, so I make it a priority.

My wife has become my helper in this process, since she knows that she will be the biggest benefactor from my spending time with the Lord. I often hear men say that their wives are the biggest impediment to quiet time. Every time the man gets up to read Scripture, the wife sees a chance to finally get him to do some task he's been putting off. So she'll mention changing the battery in the smoke alarm, which causes him to neglect his time with the Lord. It's even worse at night, since she's finally got a chance for some uninterrupted adult conversation. Rather than focusing on the Lord, they begin talking about people at work, and soon they're both too tired for reading Scripture. Wives, encourage your husbands to spend time with God, then make it easy on him by allowing him those few minutes to gain the Lord's mind.

A soldier must to be able to handle God's Word, and he won't be able to do so until he spends adequate time with the Lord. If a man can spend time in the Word each day, he'll strengthen himself for the battle and set an example that can cause many others to become strong in the Lord.

CHAPTER FIFTEEN

How to Remain Pure

I n the Marines, every time a soldier was killed, we would go through his sea-bag before sending his personal effects home. Guys had a tendency to hide things, and we didn't want somebody's mother or girlfriend to get any bad surprises added to their grief. Sometimes a guy had been looking at pornography, or writing to another woman, or doing drugs, so we would go through his stuff and cleanse it before allowing it to get sent home.

What would happen if somebody dug through your secret life? Would they find a bunch of junk that needed to be cleansed or kept secret? As soldiers, we ought to be men of purity. We should set an example to others of having a pure heart and a pure mind. That will not only make you strong in the Lord, it will help others to be strong. It's hard to find examples of purity in our impure world. Sex is everywhere, inundating us with sensual messages. It takes a brave man to say no to the momentary pleasure of sex so he can say yes to the enduring joy that comes from purity in Christ.

Solomon once said that "he who chases fantasies lacks judgment" (Proverbs 12:11). Much of the impurity with which we have contact is nothing more than a fantasy. A man may look at lewd magazines or sneak into an X-rated movie, but it can never bring him what he wants. Satan is always doing that—promising things he can't deliver. He's a liar. In John, chapter eight, Jesus called the devil the father of all lies and said these words: "When he lies, he speaks his native language." Satan tells us that in impurity we will find satisfaction, but that's never true. I've never known anyone who got involved in pornography and found fulfillment or satisfaction; they find only frustration and brokenness. If a man can guard his eye-gate, so that nothing impure enters his mind, he'll protect his integrity. Job put it this way: "I made a covenant with my eyes not to look lustfully at a girl" (Job 31:1). If we do the same, we'll protect ourselves from sin and shame. We can't be perfect, but we can be pure.

Since my eldest son was six, whenever I would travel, I would ask my boys to pray that their dad wouldn't look at a woman with her clothes off, and would never go on a date with anyone but their mother. That keeps them on my team, it introduces them to the importance of purity, and above all it brings the power of the Lord into the battle on my side. I want to set an example of purity for my sons, so that they'll know how to fight in the battle when they're older. I always walk through my hotel room and pray that I would be proud to have my sons with me. You see, many guys act as though, if they are alone, nobody is looking. They think they can get away with sin because they can't see anyone who is watching. That's a silly notion.

God, our Commanding Officer, is always watching over us. We don't "get away" with sin. It stays with us, eating away at our spiritual life and armor. Who do we think we're hiding from?

Early in my career I did a poor job for a client. I knew it was a lousy performance, and that I hadn't put the work into the case that it required, but I figured I'd just "get by" with this one easy case. When the client, Mr. Adams, looked at my work, he fired me. We had a meeting in my office, and he wasn't at all happy with the job I had done. He was a major client, and I blew it. I was a new Christian, and I knew what I'd done was wrong; I just hoped no one would find out. The senior partner of my firm was upset, but I was hoping that I could smooth it all over by doing a great job on some other case. Yet God knew about it. I wasn't fooling Him.

That same day my father was coming into town to visit me. He had an influential friend he wanted me to meet, a guy who could get me a lot of business. It seems my dad had been bragging about his son the lawyer, and he was anxious to introduce me to some big wheel in Atlanta. He came into my office at lunch time and said he had set up a luncheon meeting with his friend. I was feeling pretty low, but I agreed to go meet his friend in hopes of making up for my mistake. We sat down at a table in the restaurant, and suddenly my father said, "Hey, here comes my friend!" I looked up, and realized I was staring into the face of Mr. Adams, the guy who'd just fired me. It seems he'd never connected me to my father, so we both stood there, red-faced, while my dad bragged about my great credentials as a lawyer. It was a tough day.

I was reminded of a lesson through that experience. God knows what is going on in my mind and in my life. There's no hiding from Him. When I go into a hotel room, He's right there with me. I can't fool Him by putting my head under the pillow or turning out the lights.

Paul tells the Romans to "put to death the misdeeds of the body" (Romans 8:13), and to the Colossians he says to "set your minds on things above, not on earthly things" (Colossians 3:2). Rather than filling your mind with garbage, fill it with the things of God. "Put to death, therefore, whatever belongs to your earthly nature: sexual immorality, impurity, lust, evil desires and greed, which is idolatry. Because of these, the wrath of God is coming. You used to walk in these ways, in the life you once lived. But now you must rid yourselves of all such things as these…. Let the peace of Christ rule in your hearts….Let the word of Christ dwell in you richly" (vv. 5-8, 15, 16).

Impurity is the mark of the old man, but you aren't that old man anymore. You've been changed and made new in Jesus Christ, and your life should show it. "It is God's will that you should be holy; that you should avoid sexual immorality; that each of you should learn to control his own body in a way that is holy and honorable, not in passionate lust like the heathen, who do not know God….For God did not call us to be impure, but to live a holy life" (1 Thessalonians 4:3-5, 7). There's no beating around the bush on this matter, no hiding sin from the Lord. We are not to be known for our sin, but our holiness. "Let us behave decently, as in the daytime," Paul says in Romans 13:13-14. "Not in orgies and drunkenness, not in sexual immorality and debauchery, not in dissension and jealousy. Rather, clothe yourselves with the Lord Jesus Christ, and do not think about how to gratify the desires of the sinful nature." To clothe yourself in Christ is to invest yourself in His life, so that it is Christ who lives and not yourself. Soldiers of God need to conduct themselves accordingly. The secret to this lies in thinking not about ways to gratify the sinful nature, but about the Lord and His goodness.

I was talking with an unmarried woman who had gotten pregnant, and she was complaining about her predicament. "I can't understand it," she said to me. "We prayed before every date!" Her problem was that she wanted to blame God for her own sinful choices. If we are going to step away from immorality and toward purity, we need to take our mind off the sin and put it onto the Lord Jesus. We need to take our eyes away from the pornographic images and put them on the face of Christ.

Jesus knows what it's like to be tempted. In Hebrews chapter two we read that Christ Himself "had to be made like his brothers in every way, in order that he might become a merciful and faithful high priest in service to God, and that he might make atonement for the sins of the people. Because he himself suffered when he was tempted, he is able to help those who are being tempted." Jesus was able to endure great temptation and walk away holy. He can help us do the same.

Paul says in 1 Corinthians 10:13 that God will not allow us to be tempted beyond what we can bear. All of us can achieve victory over temptation. The key is to practice the presence of God, to set our minds on the things above, rather than on earthly things. A quick look at the temptation of Jesus explains how we can remain pure.

Matthew chapter four begins, "Then Jesus was led by the Spirit into the desert to be tempted by the devil. After fasting forty days and forty nights, he was hungry. The tempter came to him...." It's interesting that right before this incident came the baptism of Jesus by John the Baptist, in which the Spirit of God descended on Christ like a dove, and the voice of God spoke, commending Him. Right after the spiritual high came the spiritual battle. That's how Satan often works. He wants us to feel overly confident about the spiritual life, so that he can sneak in and attack. "Let him who stands take heed, lest he fall" (1 Corinthians 10:12), is the appropriate truth to apply in this situation. The most dangerous time for a soldier is right after a victory. For example, the men of Troy were sure they had defeated the soldiers of Athens. That's why they let in that wonderful victory gift of a horse—the Trojan Horse. Over-confidence in the victory led directly to their defeat.

I watched a college football player intercept a pass one time, and he got so excited about the fact that there were no opponents in front of him that he looked back over his shoulder to taunt the other team as he headed toward the goal-posts. And then he headed directly into the goal-posts, knocking himself unconscious. I can relate, because I too have gone from glory to defeat on too many occasions.

Jesus, after emerging from obscurity, soul aglow, went right from a victory into a battle. The Spirit actually led Him into the wilderness—God drove His Son into the conflict. He wanted Jesus to be on the offensive in the battle. Rather than wait for the enemy to attack, go out and meet him. But make sure you are prepared.

Jesus prepared the disciples for three years before turning them loose on the world. Paul spent roughly twelve years learning about Christ from others before stepping into leadership. He needed the preparation for the huge job God was calling him to do. The reason so many people fail in the spiritual battle is because they go in unprepared. Ephesians chapter six speaks of the various types of spiritual battle gear we are to put on, and a soldier without that protection is bound to be wounded. You see, Satan knows just how to attack people. He'll look for your strengths and weaknesses, and then he'll tempt you. Sometimes he will use an obvious weakness— if you are vulnerable to sexual temptation, he'll arrange for sexual circumstances so that he can destroy your relationship with God and eventually your faith. Other times he will try to tempt you in your area of strength. If you have charisma, he'll tempt you to use it for your own gain. If you have brains, he'll tempt you to try and manipulate others. If you're good at talking, he'll tempt you to lie so as to cover yourself. If you have administrative ability, he'll tempt you to lord your position over others. That's what the devil did with Jesus, trying to tempt Him in His faith. Make no mistake, Satan's goal is to destroy you. This is a battle to the death.

Where are you tempted? Thinking through your answer to that question can help prepare you for the battle. Which pieces of armor are not firmly in place? Take a look at Ephesians chapter six, and you'll be able to determine which area needs help. If you're weak in one spot, you can bet that's the area Satan will attack.

"The tempter came to Him and said, 'If you are the Son of God, tell these stones to become bread.' Jesus answered, 'It is written: Man shall not live by bread alone, but on every word that comes from the mouth of God'" (Matthew 4:3-4). Do you see how sneaky Satan is in his attack? "*If* you are the Son of God," he said. Satan acts as though he doubts it, like he needs some sort of proof to verify Christ's divinity. He often uses deceit to create doubt in our lives. Of Jesus, he asks to see a demonstration of bread-making. It's not that it would have been a sin for Christ to eat, but that it would have been a sin for Christ to doubt God. Reworded, the temptation sounds like this: "Why did God deprive you of bread, Jesus? Doesn't He love you? I thought you were His Son! I mean, after all, God gave manna to the Israelites in the wilderness. Why is He holding out on you? Hey, why don't you make some of your own bread? Show me you're really divine. You can do this one little thing. It's no big deal. Besides, think how bad it would be if the promised Messiah were to die of starvation before appearing to the people."

Satan tempts Jesus to be self-sufficient, to satisfy His own need rather than trusting the Father to satisfy it. But the Lord sees through the temptation and replies with Scripture. In essence, Jesus argues that it isn't food that keeps us alive, it's God. Our Heavenly Father decides who lives and who dies; it isn't based on a loaf of bread. It's as though Christ were saying, "If God wills me to live, I shall live. I won't work miracles just to make something happen that I think should happen. I'll wait upon the Lord." Jesus refused to supersede His Father. God's end doesn't justify our own means. Christ fought off the temptation by relying on Scripture and faith.

You can fight Satan the same way Jesus did. Prepare yourself for the battle by memorizing Scripture which speaks directly to your most common sin. If you struggle with impure thoughts, memorize verses that talk about the importance of keeping our mind pure. If you are often tempted to criticize, memorize verses which reflect on the positive use of our mouths. Get yourself ready to remain pure in the battle. The other thing you can do is to learn to put your trust in God. Philippians 4:19 tells us that "God will meet all your needs according to his glorious riches in Christ Jesus." If we really believe that, we won't go seeking for satisfaction anywhere else.

The temptation story goes on to read, "Then the devil took him to the holy city and had him stand on the highest point of the temple. 'If you are the Son of God,' he said, 'throw yourself down. For it is written, "He will command his angels concerning you, and they will lift you up in their hands, so that you will not strike your foot against a stone." Jesus answered him, 'It is also written: Do not put the Lord your God to the test'" (Matthew 4:5-7). The devil is sharp, and he throws an amazingly subtle temptation Christ's way. In essence, he says to Jesus, "Well, I'm still not sure if you're the Son of God. So if you can't prove it to me by making bread, get God to do a miracle to prove it. You don't have to do much—just jump."

Many of us have probably been in a situation where we decided to put God to the test. You know what it's like: "Lord, if the phone rings in the next half hour, I'll know that it's a sign...." I know of a guy who came across a travel brochure for the Philippines while praying, and took that as a "sign" that he was to become a missionary to Manila. We've all known people who have let their Bibles fall open to a random passage, then used whatever verse they pointed to as their "key" verse for leading them that day. That's dangerous. God is not a magic genie. The walk with Christ is not like reading tea leaves; it's devotion to our relationship with Him and His Word. What Satan was trying to do was to get Jesus to take an easy road to success, rather than to follow God's plan.

There were many false prophets at the time of Christ. The records show that one drowned trying to split the Jordan. Another one jumped off the temple pinnacle in an attempt to "prove" his divinity. Jesus could have done something like that at any time to become accepted by the people, and in fact He did many miracles, but primarily He came to die for our sins. The prophet Isaiah described the Lord this way: "He was despised and rejected by men, a man of sorrows, and familiar with suffering. Like one from whom men hide their faces, he was despised and we esteemed him not. Surely he took up our infirmities and carried our sorrows, yet we considered him stricken by God, smitten by him, and afflicted. But he was pierced for our transgressions, he was crushed for our iniquities; the punishment that brought us peace was upon him, and by his wounds we are healed. We all, like sheep, have gone astray, each of us has turned to his own way; and the Lord has laid on him the iniquity of us all. He was oppressed and afflicted, yet he did not open his mouth; he was led like a lamb to the slaughter, and as a sheep before her shearers is silent, so he did not open his mouth. By oppression and judgment, he was taken away. And who can speak of his descendants? For he was cut off from the land of the living; for the transgression of my people he was stricken. He was assigned a grave with the wicked, and with the rich in his death, though he had done no violence, nor was any deceit in his mouth. Yet it was the Lord's will to crush him and cause him to suffer, and though the Lord makes his life a guilt offering, he will see his offspring and prolong his days, and the will of the Lord will prosper in his hand" (Isaiah 53:3-10).

Jesus came knowing that He would die. He refused to put God to the test so that He could "prove" His divinity before His time. At first multitudes followed Him, but it soon became apparent that most were just hanging around to see the show. The true disciples of Jesus didn't come to see the miracles, but to follow the God-man. It's a stupid notion to think that you can drive 110 miles per hour on the freeway while praying, "God, save me as proof of your power." That isn't faith, it's doubt looking for proof, and that's exactly what Satan was trying to get Christ to do. Jesus rejected the temptation by three things. First, He knew where His strength was, so He knew where Satan would probably attack. Second, He knew His faith, so when confronted with twisted logic He could recognize it as such. And third, He knew His Bible, so He could argue against the temptation from God's point of view. That's a pattern every soldier in the army of God can follow.

"Again," Matthew continues in his narrative, "the devil took him to a very high mountain and showed him all the kingdoms of the world and their splendor. 'All this I will give you,' he said, 'If you will bow down and worship me'" (Matthew 4:8-9). This is Satan's most oily trick, a temptation that he uses with all of us. Rather than being the blatant, "cards on the table" device many people think, this is a sly way of tempting Jesus to sin. For you see, the devil is saying to Jesus, "If you're the Son of God, why didn't you get the world? I thought the Messiah was going to be king—what's wrong, Jesus? Is God holding out on you? I'll tell you what...I'll give you the world. It will be the same thing as he would have given you, but much easier. Trust me, I've got a shortcut."

In presenting this temptation, Satan is trying to get Jesus to take the easy way to His throne. He is coming back to reign one day, and Satan knew that, so he tried to get Jesus to accept an easier path. He wanted Christ to compromise, to wink at evil. But there is no shortcut to holiness. It requires you to follow the long path of obedience, and Satan can never deliver what God promises. The best the devil will do is a pale imitation.

God promises peace, so Satan comes up with a promise to end war. God promises love, and Satan offers sexual pleasure instead. God promises joy, and Satan arrives with drunkenness. All of the devil's schemes are mere counterfeits. He's a liar, never offering what he promised. He will keep tempting and tempting until he finds the spot at which you will yield. You will be tempted to distrust God's providential care, and he'll try to get you to believe that you are responsible for all your own success, rather than the Lord.

You'll be tempted to presume upon God, going to him just when you're in trouble and ignoring Him the rest of the time. That's dangerous, as the Jews discovered in 1 Samuel 4. Knowing they were losing the war with the Philistines, they brought the Ark of the Covenant to the front lines, hoping God would use it to magically protect the Israeli soldiers. Instead, the Ark was captured by the enemy, the high priest died of shock, and his daughter-in-law gave her son a name that describes that time: Ichabod, meaning "the glory has departed." Don't distrust God's care, and don't presume upon Him to rescue you from your own stupid mistakes. He'll forgive your sin, but you'll live with the consequences.

Finally, Satan will try to get you to fulfill your ambition in your own way, rather than God's way. He offered to Jesus an alternative route to the kingdom that had less pain, but no glory. Don't insist on your own way. Be obedient to the plan of God.

I love Christ's response to Satan: "Jesus said to him, 'Away from me, Satan! For it is written, "Worship the Lord your God, and serve him only."'" Then the devil left him, and angels came and attended him" (Matthew 4:10-11). Jesus, again using Scripture as an offensive weapon, tells Satan to get lost, and he does. That's victory! Christian, you have the power to defeat Satan. He is under your feet, according to Romans chapter sixteen, a defeated enemy. You can triumph over the devil in your own life.

Jesus and Satan cannot occupy the same heart at the same time. So, like a recovering alcoholic who decides each day that he will not take a drink, Christian soldiers prepare themselves to decide each moment to follow the Lord. It's like saying, "I love you right now, Jesus, and I'll follow you today." In God's good time, all your needs will be taken care of, so there is no reason for seeking an easy way out. Of course, it takes a brave soldier to believe God, and to walk a difficult path. But by choosing to do so, we can join in Christ's victory. We can remain pure by resisting Satan. He will flee from us in defeat. Those around you will be encouraged and emboldened by your victory, and you will be responsible for turning many lives toward maturity in Jesus Christ.

Soldier, you need to be strong, leading others into battle. You also need to be brave, setting an example of holiness for others to follow. By the power and grace of God, you can do it.

The Soldier as Servant

CHAPTER SIXTEEN

The Necessity of Obedience

I was discipled by a doctor, a guy with whom I didn't really think I had all that much in common with. He was one of those smiley guys who is always chipper in the morning, something that rubs me the wrong way. I'd stumble out of bed and barely make our early breakfast meeting, gruff, grouchy, and resenting the whole process. Then the doctor would show up with this big smile and say, "Hiya, Phil, how's it going?" I wanted to strangle him. I began thinking that this doctor had a very different life from me. I mean, we all know doctors are made of money, right? So I figured he could probably afford to be so chipper because he spent his afternoons hitting golf balls on the driving range. He didn't know how tough my life was. He couldn't understand what a chore it was for me to have to get up for a seven o'clock breakfast meeting!

Then one morning he was running a few minutes late. "Aha!" I thought to myself. "He's been lounging around in bed, taking it easy, while I knocked myself out getting here on time. I knew there was something wrong with this guy." But the doctor arrived, smiley as usual. He talked through some of my Bible study material, then we got into a discussion of my relationships at work and at home. I might have resented him, but I had to admit he brought good insight and real spiritual maturity to my problems. Also, he was willing to invest and believe in me—not a safe bet in anyone's book. Then, in the middle of our conversation, his beeper went off. He went to the phone to call his office, and when he came back he said, "Sorry, but I've got to go back to the hospital."

"Back?" I asked. I didn't know he had been to the hospital that morning.

"Yes, I was up all night with a patient—a pregnant woman who's having some severe problems—and I've got to go back. Sorry," he said with that chipper smile still in place.

I sat in stunned silence. This man had been up all night, then had come down to the restaurant to meet me, and had never uttered a word of complaint? Why? What makes a guy do that?

"Obedience," he told me. "I made a commitment to you and to the Lord. I'm not going to back out of that commitment just because it's inconvenient." Here was a doctor who "hated" lawyers, but he loved me.

That's a soldier's attitude. A soldier is not only strong, acting as a leader to others, nor is he just brave, setting an example in front of others. A soldier is tender, becoming a servant to others.

We don't get too excited about servanthood in our culture. It's demeaning and distasteful. Nobody wants to be the servant. But Christ came and set an example of servanthood. We forget that Jesus did not have to come. Mankind hadn't done such a great job of things that the Lord decided He had to reveal Himself to us. We didn't deserve to be died for, yet He was willing to die on our behalf while we were still in our sins. At the Garden of Gethsemane, Jesus in His humanity desperately wanted things to work out differently. When He prayed, "If it is possible, may this cup be taken from me," He was asking the Father to arrange some other way to save people than His own death. But in the end the God-man stayed with the plan. He said, "Yet not as I will, but as You will." Jesus was willing to be obedient, even unto death. That's the servant's job.

A servant does what he is told. He doesn't complain or argue; he obeys. Perhaps the reason we struggle so much with servanthood is because it is others-centered, and we live in a self-centered society. At the Last Supper, as the disciples sat around arguing about who was the greatest, Jesus quietly placed a towel around Himself, took a bowl of water, and began washing the feet of the twelve. This was a task normally done by the lowliest servant, yet the King of Kings was bowing down at the feet of His followers, to serve them. Outside of the cross, I think there is no more appropriate depiction of the Savior. The Son of God, who with His Father created the world, stooped down and became a servant to mankind just because He loved us. He obeyed the call of the Father because He was committed to servanthood.

Christ's entire life was one of obedience. He was baptized by John "to fulfill all righteousness" (Matthew 3:15), which means to be completely obedient to the Scriptures. He was deliberately obedient to His Father when tempted by Satan. He took the good news to small towns in the area, and He healed many, in obedient fulfillment of the prophets. After the transfiguration, when Peter tried to dissuade Jesus from obedience to death, the Lord rebuked the attempt and blamed it on Satan. Jesus was determined to be obedient.

John's gospel tells us that Jesus was obedient to being sent by the Father, to teaching the Father's truth, and to serving on the Father's behalf. Christ never did what He wanted, but what God wanted. It was the authority and will of the Father that was manifested in the life of Christ. And God rewarded the Son's obedience by commending Him at His baptism, witnessing to His authority at the transfiguration, raising Him from the dead, and putting Him in charge of all things for eternity. Jesus once prayed, "I have brought you glory on earth by completing the work you gave me to do" (John 17:4). He was obedient in all things, and that brought glory to God.

Every Christian is either living in obedience or living in rebellion. There is no middle ground. The Bible offers a number of examples of men who were faced with the choice of obeying or disobeying God. Abel chose to obey God in worship by offering a blood sacrifice, while Cain chose to disobey and offer God the work of his own hands. Noah chose to obey God and heed His word, while the people of Noah's day decided to ignore the warnings of God. When Abraham disobeyed God by trying to create his own offspring through Hagar, he suffered consequences that are still felt today. But when Abraham obeyed God, he was blessed with a son; from his lineage the entire world was blessed. Abraham learned the importance of obedience, so that when God asked him to sacrifice his son, Abraham was willing to obey.

Sometimes God works that way. He asks us to do the impossible. We are called to obey an incredibly hard command, and we must decide if we'll obey or rebel. Gideon was called to attack a vast army with three hundred men. It must have seemed a suicidal command, but Gideon obeyed and was handed an incredible victory. Moses, a shepherd whose temper had run him out of the Egyptian elite, was asked to free two million people, then lead them on a cross-country march. He obeyed, and he got to meet God face to face. Joshua was called not to attack Jericho, but to march around its walls and shout. He could have disobeyed, planning instead a frontal assault on the city, but Joshua chose to obey the Lord. He was given one of the most memorable military victories of all time. When God calls you to do the impossible, obey Him. He has the power to do immeasurably more than all you can imagine, and that power is at work inside of you.

A soldier obeys his commanding officer, even if it seems impossible. The soldier's job isn't to argue about tactics, but to implement the plan. Obedience is linked to trust, because the soldier must trust that the commanding officer recognizes the situation and knows what action will best accomplish the goals.

God sometimes calls His soldiers to be obedient in the face of danger. Daniel chose to pray to God, with his window open, even though he knew the practice had been banned. For his obedience he got thrown into a lion's den. Daniel's three friends, Shadrach, Meshach, and Abednego, chose to obey God rather than bow before an idol. They knew that their decision to obey God could cost them their lives, but they said, "If we are thrown into the blazing furnace, the God we serve is able to save us from it, and he will rescue us from your hand, O king. But even if he does not, we want you to know, O king, that we will not serve your gods or worship the image of gold you have set up" (Daniel 3:17-18). Of course, the Lord delivered both Daniel and his friends, but they didn't know for certain that would happen. They were willing to obey even if it cost them their lives.

That's the attitude of a soldier. We go into battle even though we know we are targets and might get wounded. My father's generation marched bravely into the fighting in

Europe and the Pacific, even though it was clear many would die. They simply believed in the cause. They trusted the leadership, so they obeyed. Sometimes I wonder what would happen to our country if we were faced with another war such as that. Would young men still be willing to fight and die, or do they believe there is even a cause worth dying for? In an age of skepticism and self-centeredness, would our people be willing to respond to authority?

A soldier understands the need to obey. One of the scariest battle scenes in our country's history occurred on December 13, 1862, just outside the city of Fredericksburg, Virginia. Confederate forces were in entrenched positions on high ground, but the Union forces decided to attack anyway. Massed artillery and a four-foot-high stone fence allowed the Southerners to station four lines of infantry behind good cover. As row after row of Union soldiers advanced toward them, they walked straight into a withering fire, sheets of lead pouring from unbroken volleys. Yet on and on they came, only to be mowed down by more and more fire. A Southern general referred to the felling of Union soldiers at Fredericksburg as a "steady dripping of rain from the eaves of a house."

I picture myself as one of the soldiers in the back. As row after row of my comrades move forward, and I see all of them fall before the enemy, would I have been able to obey? What moves men to march onto a field knowing that they are about to be shot? The soldiers at Fredericksburg were some of the most heroic and obedient of the Civil War. You may shake your head at the horror of war, but you've got to marvel at their courageous obedience.

We are the servants of God, called to obey Him in all things. If we will obey, God will bless us and use us. Moses told his people, "If you fully obey the Lord your God and carefully follow all his commands I give you today, the Lord your God will set you high above all the nations on earth. All these blessings will come upon you and accompany you if you obey the Lord" (Deuteronomy 28:1-2). The people in Scripture didn't obey God for merely practical reasons, but God did bless their obedience. "Blessed are they whose ways are blameless, who walk according to the law of the Lord," says the Psalmist. "Blessed are they who keep his statutes and seek him with all their heart. They do nothing wrong; they walk in his ways. You have laid down precepts that are to be fully obeyed" (Psalm 119:1-4).

In the Marine Corps, I learned the tremendous principle of minding orders without question. I wanted to instill that principle in our children, so when they were old enough to walk, I worked on helping them understand the importance of coming to me when I called them, and stopping whatever they were doing when I said, "Stop." I wasn't militaristic about this, and I tried to offer a lot of encouragement and affirmation when they minded me. One time, at a CBMC picnic, our small children began to wander off toward the big field close by. The people were amazed to see my five-year-old daughter stop when I said, "Abigail, please stop." They were even more amazed that she came right to me when I said, "Abigail, please come here." One guy even said, "Phil, I'd like you to train my bird-dogs to do that!"

The principle of obedience has always been a part of my life and our family. Many times I've felt the Spirit of God say to me, "Stop!" and I knew I had to obey. If we're going to be soldiers, we'll have to learn to obey when our Commanding Officer tells us to "Stop"—or to "Go!"

"To obey is better than sacrifice," it says in 1 Samuel 15:22. We obey because we are commanded to obey by God, who loves us and is our King. David urged us to obey because God made us, so we owe Him our lives. We are under an obligation to obey Him, since Christ has died for us to give us life. As Paul says to the Corinthians, "You were bought at a price. Therefore honor God with your body" (1 Corinthians 6:20).

It was out of obedience that I began praying for the Lord to give me a heart for people. My experience had always led me to either use people or run by them, but I wanted to see people the way Christ saw people because we've been commanded to love them. I didn't pray for selfish reasons, but because I wanted to obey, and God responded to my obedience by filling my heart with love. In the same way, Susy was willing to forgive me all my failings because she knew she was commanded to forgive. She may not have felt like forgiving me, but she wanted to be obedient to the Lord, and God was gracious in filling her heart with a renewed love for me. There are plenty of times I have not wanted to obey the Lord, but the more I do, the more peace and joy I find in Him.

It is possible to obey God outwardly, while inwardly rebelling against Him. True obedience is more than merely subjecting yourself to God's leadership—it's responding to the Lord in love. A person can be subservient on the outside and never develop an inner desire for obedience, but a servant learns to obey both internally and externally. His outward activity is inseparable from his inner assent.

Jesus criticized those who put on an appearance of obeying while retaining a rebellious heart. "Woe to you, teachers of the law and Pharisees, you hypocrites! You give a tenth of your spices—mint, dill and cumin—but you have neglected the more important matters of the law—justice, mercy and faithfulness. You should have practiced the latter, without neglecting the former....You clean the outside of the cup and dish, but inside they are full of greed and self-indulgence" (Matthew 23:23, 25). Soldiers can be disciplined for something called "silent defiance"—the rebellion in his heart which reveals itself in his attitude. As Christians, we are not only soldiers but servants, obeying the Lord out of a heart of love.

Obedience is the mark of your personal decision to trust God and commit your life to Him. You can recognize a soldier of God by his willingness to serve. As the Lord said, "My mother and brothers are those who hear God's word and put it into practice" (Luke 8:21). Paul put it this way: "Don't you know that when you offer yourselves to someone to obey him as slaves, you are slaves to the one whom you obey—whether you are slaves to sin, which leads to death, or to obedience, which leads to righteousness? But thanks be to God that, though you used to be slaves to sin, you wholeheartedly obeyed the form of teaching to which you were entrusted. You have been set free from sin and have become slaves to righteousness" (Romans 6:16-18). Your obedience to God reveals that you are his slave.

My family needs to see my obedience to God so that they know I'm not a hypocrite. If my son hears me talk about reading the Bible, he'd better see me reading it so he doesn't think I'm just blowing smoke. I've got to be openly obedient, so that those around me can see my faith is real. My obedience will reveal things about my character.

An obedient soldier shows himself as being wise: "Everyone who hears these words of mine and puts them into practice is like a wise man who built his house on the rock. The rain came down, the steams rose, and the winds blew and beat against that house; yet it did not fall, because it had its foundation on the rock" (Matthew 7:24-25). In other words, my obedience to the Lord and His Word will change my life by giving me peace, wisdom, and assurance. Beyond that, it will impact the lives of those around you by proving your sincere faith to others. Your obedience and service will cause people to turn to God. "Because of the service by which you have proved yourselves," Paul explains to the Corinthians, "men will praise God for the obedience that accompanies your confession of the gospel of Christ" (2 Corinthians 9:13).

Soldiers are not just warriors, but servants to their commanding officer. They prove their wisdom and value by obedience. May our lives be marked by that sort of obedience.

CHAPTER SEVENTEEN

Focused on the Battle

U riah was probably sharpening his weapon during a respite from the fighting when the messenger arrived. "The king wants to see you," he was told.

"The king? Me?" Uh-oh. Something must be up. "Why would our king want to talk with me?"

"Get moving."

So Uriah left behind his friends and fellow warriors, and travelled with a small team of well-armed men back to the castle. He had a mixture of excitement and fear inside him —excitement that he might be getting promoted, fear that something was wrong. Uriah wasn't the sort of guy who normally hung around with kings. He was a soldier, who loved his wife and his country, and fought to protect them. He didn't like leaving his squad; they had become close. They fought for one another, and would do anything to protect their partners. There was a bond that held them together as soldiers, and Uriah knew that the other guys would resent his leaving, while at the same time wishing they could return to Jerusalem for a visit. Fighting in wars was an ugly business in those days, and it made men hard. All the way back to the capitol, Uriah asked people if they knew why he had been summoned to meet the king.

The mystery grew deeper as he entered the king's palace. Instead of meeting with a team of military advisers, Uriah was called into King David's personal quarters, where they had a one-on-one chat. There was no promotion, but neither was there any problem. The king had looked him over, rather nervously Uriah thought, and then asked, "How is Joab?" Uriah replied that Joab was fine, so far as he knew. He served in a different company from Joab, so he wasn't really sure. The king walked around, as though he was thinking of something else, then he asked, "And how are the soldiers?"

"They fight hard for their king," Uriah replied, wondering what King David wanted. They had been out for a few weeks, battling the enemy, and Uriah felt he still had much to learn about war, but he kept those thoughts to himself. Some of the men had complained that this time the king had not come with them, but Uriah was sure he didn't want to share any of that talk with David. There was a war going on, and here he was making small talk with his commander-in-chief. Then the king, still nervously pacing, asked him another question: "How do you think the war is going?"

Now Uriah knew something was up. Kings don't ask average soldiers like himself for their advice on war. He tried to think of the right way of answering the king's query, but decided the best response was to be short and positive. "It goes well," he said, satisfied with the vagueness of his answer. The king stared at him for a few moments, nodded, then said in a rather matter-of-fact tone, "Well, go down to your house and wash your feet. I'm sure your wife is waiting for you."

Uriah didn't know what to think. Was this a test? Surely he hadn't been called all the back from the front line just to make small talk with the King of Israel. He was glad to be back in Jerusalem, but he had no plans to go home. That wouldn't be fair to the rest of the men in his company. His job was to be out of the field of battle with the other men, fighting for his homeland, not taking it easy at home. Uriah had too much honor for that.

Not knowing what else to do, Uriah hung around the royal palace until dark, then slept in the doorway of the palace with the servants. If he was going to be a soldier, he knew there were no part-time soldiers, so he did as any professional soldier would do. The next day he was summoned back into the king's room. This time Uriah was hoping for some clue as to why he had been brought back from the fighting.

As soon as he entered the room, King David was talking to him. "Haven't you just come a great distance?" the king asked.

"Yes," replied Uriah.

"Then why didn't you go home?"

Perhaps the king wanted to test him, to see how he would respond when challenged. Uriah, not sure what the king was fishing for, decided it was best to simply tell the truth. "The Ark and Israel and Judah are staying in tents, and my master Joab and my lord's men are camped in open fields. How could I go to my house to eat and drink and lie with my wife? As surely as you live, I will not do such a thing." He was a simple man, and the unvarnished truth revealed his character. Uriah wanted to be fair to others, and assumed others would be fair to him. The king just looked at him with a mixture of frustration and anxiety.

"Stay here one more day," the king finally said, "and tomorrow I will send you back."

Uriah still had no idea what the king wanted, but he figured one more day of waiting wouldn't be too bad, so he thanked the king and went out. That night, at David's invitation, he joined the king for drinks, and the two talked about all kinds of things while downing a bit too much wine. He was feeling a little tipsy as he left the dining room, but Uriah had enough control over himself to once again protect his integrity by sleeping on the mat outside the palace door. The next morning he didn't get to see the king, but was sent back to the battle lines with Joab, who kept looking at him strangely.

You can't help but feel sorry for Uriah. He was a soldier, uninvolved in civilian pursuits. His job was to serve king and country. Uriah's focus was on the war. There wasn't even a second place in his mind.

David's focus should have been on the war, but instead it was on a beautiful woman he had seen one night while walking the parapet of his palace. He was more interested in his own pleasure than in the fighting his countrymen were doing. Then the woman got pregnant, so King David had brought her husband Uriah back, to cover up the sin. Uriah's response: "I will not do this thing." He was a soldier, first and last, and that meant holding to a soldier's code. Uriah had his integrity to maintain; David had already lost his. I've often wondered what David said to Uriah when they came face-to-face in the presence of God.

God wants us focused on the battle. We are His soldiers, and a soldier thinking about something else is completely worthless in a fight. Not only are we God's soldiers, we are His servants, serving at His command. God is in the battle of the ages, fighting Satan and his forces all over this world. The devil has vowed to destroy us. If you lose your focus, you can lose the battle.

There are a number of people in our world who have lost their focus. Too many guards have fallen asleep while on watch. Fathers are sitting in front of television sets, allowing their sons to be shaped by peers or the media rather than doing the job themselves. Occasionally they'll toss a piece of advice to their sons, but it doesn't take long for the boys to figure out that the advice is simply good intention, not principles for living. The dad will say, "Don't get involved in pornography, son, it'll ruin your life." Then he'll end the lecture by flipping on the TV set to catch the rerun of *Baywatch*. He'll sing in church about it being well with his soul, but then model to his boys that anger is an acceptable way to let off steam, or get your own way, or end a conversation. Or he'll come home from work mad because his boss corrected him, and start talking about the "battle" he is in at work.

But the battle isn't with his job or his boss or his co-workers. The battle is with Satan. If your boss doesn't know Jesus Christ, you'll have to battle Satan to win him to the Lord. And we can't expect this to be a fair fight. There isn't going to be much fairness or agreement with the world—they're the slaves of the enemy, blinded and duped by Satan. You've got to win them to Christ if you expect things to change. You've got to stay focused on the battle if you expect to achieve a victory.

The pressures of my law practice were instrumental in my seeking and then coming to Christ, since I was seeking peace from the stress of my work. Once I became a Christian, I assumed God would turn me into a missionary and send me to Africa (as a matter of fact, there were times I pleaded with Him to do exactly that!). Of course, God did make me a missionary, but He sent me to the place for which I was best trained. I already knew the language, had the right clothes, and had a position of authority to reach the central business district of Atlanta, Georgia. The Lord in His wisdom called me to minister to that particular mission field. My next fifteen years were dedicated to serving Him in one of the most needy and influential mission fields in the world—the marketplace.

I once lectured a friend with marital troubles on the evils of divorce. Rather than convincing him, I alienated him from God. The issue was Jesus, not divorce, but I allowed myself to get off track. As Christians, we're not the morality police. We can't expect regenerate behavior from unregenerate people. Sure, there will be instances where we will have to stand up for morality and justice and truth, but we don't want to alienate people. We want to win them. The battle is not to change the language of the people we work with. The battle is not to change the laws of our culture. The battle is to change lives by introducing others to Jesus Christ. The people around you are not the enemy; they're the victims of the enemy.

Husband, your wife is not the enemy. Even though she nags you and always seems to disapprove of the things you do, she's not the enemy. Wife, that competitive guy you married, who wants to win every argument and takes every comment as criticism, isn't the enemy. Don't treat him like he is.

Instead, stay focused on the battle, and serve your partner. Think about what the problem is between the two of you, and pray that God can bring about reconciliation. But don't mistake your spouse for the enemy. Satan is the enemy, and he's trying to destroy you. If you don't stay focused on the battle, you can lose that perspective.

Your spouse is your partner in battle; accept her as part of your soul-winning team. You can't expect her to successfully raise children in an evil age and weather the warfare of Satan, unless you are a team. Your spouse needs to be your closest confidant, who knows what you need and understands how to pray for you. In battle, she ought to be your first choice as a partner. Remember, she'll hurt when you get wounded, so be willing to protect her with your own life. A husband and wife who aren't in the battle together are not at full strength, and probably too preoccupied with their own relationship to be focused on the battle.

Take some time together to map out your strategy. What are the goals you have for your family and your relationship? What are each person's strengths and weaknesses? Make sure you know how to go into battle together—a team is much more dangerous to the enemy than an individual. One thing I've learned in business is that a Chief Executive Officer who fails to meet with his staff to make a plan will soon be out of work. You've got to communicate with one another if you're going to be focused on the battle.

I've seen too many men in ministry forget about their families, then have their ministries crumble because of the weakness in their family life. You can't just drop your wife and kids to fight by yourself; you fight together. The prophet Jeremiah spoke of fathers in the midst of battle who hear the sound of approaching steeds, and "at the noise of enemy chariots and the rumble of their wheels, fathers will not turn to help their children; their hands will hang limp" (Jeremiah 47:3). Rather than taking the approach that, as a soldier, they are servants dedicated to protecting their families, these fathers were too afraid to do anything in battle. They stood by and watched their children get slaughtered.

It's happening with Christian men today. Their sons are involved with the culture rather than Christ. Their daughters are more concerned with fashion and popularity than holiness and morality. We can't afford to lose a generation of believers. Satan wants to destroy our children as much as he wants to destroy us, so we've got to be focused on the battle. That means setting an example in front of our kids, letting them see Christ at work in us. It means making them part of our team, allowing them to see us in daily devotions, talking with them about the faith, and letting them experience our ministry.

I remember getting so busy with my schedule that I couldn't fit everything into my calendar. I even complained to my wife, "Susy, I don't have time for my devotions or the man I'm discipling. I've got too many things to do for the ministry."

Her response to me? "Phil, that is the ministry."

She's right. Having me spend time in the Word so that I grow to know God and see Him at work in me, then sharing that faith with someone else, is what my ministry is all about. If I give up on those to take care of administrative details, we might as well fold up the tents, because CBMC will have become a useless social organization. I want to stay focused on the battle, and that will mean continuing to do those things that I know are crucial to our effectiveness. It means doing the things that make us strong and prepared for the spiritual battle.

Some people never seem to get into the war. They'll offer some excuse for putting off the decision to focus on the battle. I remember saying in high school, "When I get to college, I'll start to study." I didn't study in high school, and I flunked too many courses, but I put off doing anything that would actually prepare me for college. Then when I arrived at college, I flunked out because I wasn't ready. I remember saying during college, "When I get married, I won't lust." But I never took the time to prepare myself for holiness and commitment to my wife, so when I got married I continued my destructive thought life. What we do now prepares us for the future, so if we fail to plan we might as well plan to fail. I see would-be soldiers saying, "When I get into the battle, I'll have discipline. There'll be no more goofing off for me!" But without preparation, these guys are going to get severely wounded in battle. It takes training, commitment, and dedication to fight effectively. It takes someone willing to put away childish things and focus on the battle.

There are four things every new soldier should work on to help him focus on the spiritual war. First, he needs to develop passion. In Acts 4:31 the first believers got together to prepare themselves in prayer, and the whole house shook by the power of the Holy Spirit. They must have had tremendous passion to see that kind of response from God, and it showed in that they "spoke the Word of God boldly." The gospels tell us that Jesus would often rise up before dawn to be alone with the Lord, and Luke 6:12 says that He stayed up praying all night. As a matter of fact, Hebrews 7:25 says Christ is still praying for us. If you want to develop passion in your life, spend time in prayer. If you want to see revival in your church and neighborhood, spend time in prayer. There aren't any gimmicks to developing passion. Just pray. "Pray in the Spirit on all occasions with all kinds of prayers and requests," Paul tells the Ephesians. Put everything into your prayers. Develop passion through prayer. All the great events in Christendom have come after fervent, focused prayer.

The second element of preparation that you need is purity. If you really want to find yourself becoming strong and brave for God, develop a lifestyle of obedience to Him. Live a pure life. Psalm 145:18 says, "The Lord is near to all who call on him in truth." Sin in your life hinders your prayers, but obedience fosters prayer. People talk about going into battle today, but they don't want to make the necessary lifestyle changes to prepare themselves. Look to develop purity in your life.

The third step in preparing yourself for battle is to develop persistence. Paul regularly spoke of his persistence in prayer, and how it prepared him for the daily war. To the Ephesians he wrote, "Ever since I heard about your faith in the Lord Jesus and your love for all the saints, I have not stopped giving thanks for you remembering you in my prayers." To the believers at Colossae, he said, "Since the day we heard about you, we have not stopped praying for you and asking God to fill you with the knowledge of his will through all spiritual wisdom and understanding." To the church in Rome he wrote, "God, whom I serve with my whole heart in preaching the gospel of His Son, is my witness how constantly I remember you in my prayers at all times." And to the Christians in Thessalonica he said, "Night and day we pray most earnestly that we may see you again and supply what is lacking in your faith." The Christian life is one of persistence; doing the hard work again and again. Spending persistent time in prayer will help prepare you by giving you the determination required for the battle.

The last thing I'll recommend is to develop a positive faith in your prayer life. Don't just pray for the easy things, or the things you know will occur. Pray for something big. Jesus once said to His disciples, "Therefore I tell you, whatever you ask for in prayer, believe that you have received it, and it will be yours" (Mark 11:24). Spend time reading God's Word to build your faith, then hit your knees in prayer and ask the Lord to move mountains. Remember, "faith comes from hearing the message, and the message is heard through the word of Christ" (Romans 10:17). So if you want to prepare yourself for the spiritual war, spend time reading your Bible to develop great faith. When you see how dependable the Lord has been in the past, you'll develop a confident assurance that He will be with you in the future.

If you'll take the time to develop passion, purity, persistence, and positive faith, you'll be prepared to do battle for the cause of Christ. Paul reminded Timothy that soldiers aren't concerned with civilian pursuits. They are focused on the battle. On what are you focused?

CHAPTER EIGHTEEN

Serving Under Authority

A s soldiers, we serve under the authority of the King. I love the story of the Centurion, who marched up to Jesus and said, "My servant lies at home paralyzed and in terrible suffering." Jesus offered to go and heal the man's servant, but that Roman soldier, who was in charge of one hundred other soldiers, replied, "Lord, I do not deserve to have you come under my roof. But just say the word, and my servant will be healed. For I myself am a man under authority, with soldiers under me. I tell this one, 'Go,' and he goes; and that one, 'Come,' and he comes. I say to my servant, 'Do this,' and he does it" (Matthew 8:8-9). That Centurion understood the value of authority.

Christ is the head of the church. The head carries out its functions through the body, so Christ works through us to accomplish His purposes. Just as there is a mutual dependence between the physical head and the body, so there is between Christ and His church. He is dependent upon His soldiers as the medium for expressing Himself and accomplishing His goals, and His soldiers are dependent upon Him for wisdom and direction in doing that. Christ is dependent upon His army to do His work; and His army is dependent upon Him for the power to do it. We are under His authority, working as His servants in the world.

Have you ever met someone who has given his life completely to the Lord? It's both exciting and faith-building. We spoke with a couple one time who said, "We are willing to go anywhere and do anything to serve God." And they meant it. God has called them into a brutal ministry, but they are obedient to the call and the Lord is using them to raise up an army of soul-winners.

I am a man under authority. God called me to the presidency of Christian Business Men's Committee, and I had to obey. There are times I don't feel adequate for the role, but that's not my concern. God put me here, so if there's a problem, you'll have to take it up with Him!

My wife is a woman under authority. She works hard educating and equipping our children to be Christians in a non-Christian world. Susy wasn't trained for that role; she was trained as a corporate lawyer, but she says that she is content because all she wants to do is please her Commanding Officer, Jesus Christ. Serving the Lord is never easy. We have to learn to be comfortable in the place God calls us, and that takes maturity.

Susy is modeling that principle to our children as demonstrated by the following poem written by our thirteen year old son:

The Peasant Soldier

I am just a peasant, of the age of thirteen,
I'd never fought in battle, nor one ever had I seen.
But one day all that changed, and soon we will see
How a mere farmer joined the King's infantry.
When I first heard the rumor, I thought it was a ruse.
Then my friend told me it was legitimate news,
That an army was coming with sword, spear, and helm,
To attack, conquer, and burn the King's Realm.
I went to the King's men at the foremost gate
Hoping to be of service. I was told to wait.
Then an officer came out and said, "What did you bring?
Allow it to be used in service to your King."
I gave him my knife which was all I had to give.
'Twas a costly gift when on a farm you live.
Satisfied, he turned to walk quickly away
When I said, "Sir, that is not all I wish to give today.
I wish to give myself to fight beside your men
So that peace may come to this land once again."
At first he looked surprised,
Then 'cross his face spread a smile.
And he said, "I've not seen such bravery from a peasant in a while!"
Then he took me to the armory and gave me shield and sword,
And also a crimson cape that seemed fit for a Castle Lord.
Calling a captain over he told him of my deeds,
Then in conclusion he said, "Captain, this man, the King's army needs.
Later in the week it happened, when the enemy army came,
That I was fighting with the King's men amidst steel and flame.
In the end the enemy was routed and they fled in desperation.
Seeing this, the Castle erupted in celebration!
Perhaps mine was the voice that the loudest did ring,
For I, a peasant had fought for the King!

Paul Downer
June 1, 1996

David Brainerd was a nineteen-year-old boy who felt called by God to take the gospel of Jesus Christ to the American Indians. The call made no sense to anyone. The year was 1737, and the vast wilderness of North America made for a harsh lifestyle. The boy knew no Indians, did not speak their language, and had no apparent skills for surviving in the wild. But he was a man under authority, so he obeyed the call of God. He went out to preach the good news, and in ten years led ten thousand Indians to a saving knowledge of Jesus Christ. He died at the age of twenty-nine of tuberculosis, brought on by exposure to the severe winters of the American landscape. To everyone else, David Brainerd's calling seemed insane. To a man under authority, it was an order to be obeyed.

Bruce Olson was also nineteen years old when he left his Minnesota home and traveled to South America. He was a man under authority, called to preach the gospel to a particular tribe living in the mountains between Venezuela and Colombia. He had no mission agency supporting him, nor even the backing of supportive parents. He didn't speak their language, and in fact no one had ever survived contact with that tribe. But he had his orders, so Bruce Olson obeyed. Though severely wounded in his first contact with the tribe, he eventually befriended them, joined a village, and led many to a saving knowledge of Christ. His ministry profoundly changed their culture.

As men under authority, we are often asked to do hard things. Peter was asked to preach in the courtyard of the Jewish temple in Jerusalem. Paul was asked to preach in the courtyard of the pagan deities in Athens. Martin Luther was asked to preach the truth in the face of an apostate church. Mother Theresa was asked to share the love of Jesus with the poor and the sick of India. Christians have always been asked by God to do the hard things.

It is not easy to serve under authority. My ego doesn't like it. My natural inclination is to have people notice me and tell me what a great job I'm doing, what a valuable person I am to the team. But in God's army, all the glory goes to Him. I wouldn't have the power to do anything if it were not for the power of God flowing through me. I wouldn't have the wisdom to fight in the battle if it were not for the Spirit guiding and teaching me. There is only one star in the church, and it's Jesus Christ.

Timothy understood that. He was content to be Paul's co-pilot, serving under Christ's authority no matter what sort of opposition he faced. You've also got to admire Paul's attitude. He didn't seem to care who got the credit, so long as Christ was proclaimed. A principle of administration that I see at work in Paul's life is this: You'll be amazed how much you can accomplish if you don't care who gets the credit. Paul was a man under authority, serving the Lord Jesus wherever and whenever he was called. His service kept him close to the Lord. "The eyes of the Lord are on those who fear Him, on those whose hope is in his unfailing love" (Psalm 33:18).

Paul once asked a man under his authority to do something hard. Philemon was a Greek man who had moved to the city of Colossae and gotten rich. He had met Paul and became a Christian, and his life had changed radically. Others looked to him for leadership. His life was a testimony, and his faith in God and love for Christians was widely recognized. His wife, Apphia, a woman from Phyrgia, had also become a Christian, and the local church met in their home.

Philemon owned slaves, as did most wealthy businessmen of his day. There were approximately one hundred and twenty million people in the Roman empire, and it is estimated that half of them were slaves. Those slaves were sometimes treated poorly, but sometimes treated very well, as though they were members of the family. A man who owed money could indenture himself to his master until he could pay off his account, and many chose to remain in slavery because their prospects for work outside the home were poor. The two classes of people, slave and master, sometimes hated each other. If a slave ran away, his penalty upon being caught was death.

One of Philemon's slaves, a man named Onesimus, had run away. He had apparently been a poor worker, as Paul referred to him as "useless" to Philemon. Yet while Onesimus was running, he ran into another slave: Paul, who was a slave for Christ. Paul was serving time in prison for preaching about Jesus, and Onesimus heard him. Eventually that run-away slave gave his life to Jesus Christ, and admitted his sin to Paul. Consider the amazing situation for a moment: The Lord had worked out the circumstances so that one runaway slave, in an empire of sixty million slaves, met up with the man who had led his former master to Jesus Christ. Paul, seeing a wonderful opportunity to teach his friend about authority, wrote to Philemon to tell him of his newest convert.

"I am sending him—who is my very heart—back to you. I would have liked to keep him with me so that he could take your place in helping me while I am in chains for the gospel. But I did not want to do anything without your consent, so that any favor you do will be spontaneous and not forced. Perhaps the reason he was separated from you for a little while was that you might have him back for good—no longer as a slave, but better than a slave, as a dear brother. He is very dear to me but even dearer to you, both as a man and as a brother in the Lord" (Philemon 12-16). Paul sent Onesimus back to his owner, not because he wanted to, but because Philemon was the legal owner. Paul could have tried to coerce Philemon to give him up, but he didn't want to do that. He wanted Philemon, a man under authority, to decide for himself. Would he live out the gospel? Would he forgive and do what is right?

Put yourself in Philemon's place for a moment. A successful businessman, he was offended and embarrassed at the actions of his slave. Besides that, as a slave, Onesimus left a lot to be desired. This guy deserved punishment. Philemon had every right to punish him.

But God's hand was in this. Onesimus had become a brother in Christ. Paul wrote to say, "He is my brother. How will you treat my brother?" It was a tough call for everyone involved, and you've got to appreciate the obedience at work in this situation.

Onesimus was a man under authority. He faced death by being obedient and returning to his master. He didn't know the outcome of that decision.

Philemon also was a man under authority. He was known for his love for the brothers, but suddenly he was being asked to forgive a man who had publicly offended him. If he forgave Onesimus, he didn't know how that decision would effect his other slaves or his standing in the community.

And Paul was a man under authority. Both of these men owed their eternal destiny to him, but he was willing to say to Philemon, "If he has done you any wrong or owes you anything, charge it to me. I, Paul, am writing this with my own hand. I will pay it back" (vv. 18-19). He was asking a big favor, but he requests that Philemon "refresh" his heart by granting Onesimus forgiveness. "Confident of your obedience," Paul concluded, "I write to you, knowing that you will do even more than I ask."

Living the gospel demands tough obedience. None of these men had easy choices. Onesimus could have said nothing, but then he would never have had his integrity. Paul could have failed to tell his friend, but then his ministry would have been compromised by his lack of integrity. Philemon had a difficult choice, having to forgive and treat like a brother the lazy slave who had run away and shamed him. These were all men under authority, and the Lord put this story in our Scriptures to remind us of that fact. Being a soldier is never easy. It means having to serve others. Each of these men in turn became the servant to the other. That's one of the roles of soldiering.

Friend, you too are a man under authority. God may be calling you to do something difficult, but if you do not obey Him, you'll never be used effectively in His army.

CHAPTER NINETEEN

A Servant is Humble

L ife has a tendency to deliver humbling circumstances. A friend of mine was once late for a political speech, so when he got to the conference center he didn't wait to explain himself to anyone. He just raced by the registration tables, ran to the front, and began talking to the crowd. He couldn't understand the confused looks on their faces. When somebody up front tried to get his attention, he waved them off and kept going. Eventually a guy came over to him and placed his hand over the microphone, forcing my friend to stop speaking.

"Can I ask you a question?" the man asked. "Who are you and why are you blabbering about politics?"

Flustered, my friend replied that he'd been asked to speak to the Republicans in town.

"Well that's fine," the other man responded, "except this is the Western States RV-owners conference." Then pointing out the door, he added, "You might want to try that other room."

Many of us have experienced something similar. Life keeps us humble, and many people's self-esteem can't tolerate that kind of humility. That's why they chafe at the idea of humbly serving the Lord Jesus when they would rather serve their own desires. One of the reasons God's people will be different in this world is because of their humility.

Look around you. Do you see much humility in our culture? Movies are filled with messages of self-pleasure, television is dominated with advertisements and story lines that are self-centered, and magazine advertisements are designed to make you self-conscious. Into that sort of culture comes Jesus Christ, who says that we are to be humble, and it goes against everything people believe to be true.

In Philippians 2:8 we read that Christ "humbled himself and became obedient to death—even death on a cross." Humility and obedience go hand in hand. His soldiers serve Him in humility.

Most men find their identity in their careers. Their jobs define them, so when they introduce themselves to each other the first question that's asked, after the exchange of names, is, "What do you do?" Their entire persona is wrapped up in a job or a business. That's scary, because if a man like that loses his job, he loses his identity. On many occasions I have met men who are so wrapped up in their businesses that they take the loss of their family easier than the loss of their career. Humility is close by, particularly in this age of downsizing. Your job or your company can be ripped from your hands, and suddenly you don't know who you are. Strangely enough, that sort of humbling circumstance is often used by God to shape our character. When a man has been humbled, he will respond either by becoming hard or by becoming tender.

A hard man has his pride hurt, and he can look to no one's interests but his own. That allows him to pull back from other relationships so as to keep from getting hurt. He may, by his own strength of will, go on to great success in some other field, but he'll never develop a heart for other people. He'll succeed just to spite those who hurt him. Other men will fall apart, blame others for their position, and shut everyone out. They'll never find success, because they'll seldom try again.

But a man who had been made tender because of his humbling circumstances will respond very differently. He'll develop a heart for other people. Having felt their pain, he will seek to assist others who go through hard times. It may sound odd, but Christ wants His soldiers to be strong and brave, but also to be tender, thinking of the needs of others. He wants us to be thinking about the concerns of others, sensitive to their position. We are to be humble, serving the King. "Let not the wise man boast of his wisdom or the strong man boast of his strength or the rich man boast of his riches, but let him who boasts boast about this: that he understands and knows me, that I am the Lord, who exercises kindness, justice and righteousness on earth, for in these I delight, declares the Lord" (Jeremiah 9:23-24).

Men, learn to delight in God rather than your job. Learn to find your identity in Christ and His work rather than in your own work. For you see, your work doesn't matter all that much in light of eternity, but Christ's work will stand for all time. When you recognize who you are in comparison to the Lord Jesus, you won't think so highly of yourself. It's amazing, but every time someone comes face to face with God, he recognizes his own inadequacy. When the prophet Isaiah saw the Lord, he immediately fell on his face and exclaimed, "Woe is me, for I am a man of unclean lips!" Isaiah was struck by the contrast between the holiness of God and his own sinfulness—an amazing thought, when you consider that Isaiah was God's spokesman to His people.

When Peter first met the Lord, he was fishing. Christ encouraged Peter to throw out his nets again, but Peter didn't want to do it. "We've worked hard all night, and haven't caught anything, but if you say so...." With the next toss of the nets, they caught so many fish that the nets began breaking. Did Peter respond by praising God? Did he celebrate that a true prophet must have arrived? No, he fell on his knees and said, "Go away from me, Lord; for I am a sinful man!" In recognizing the person of Jesus, Peter became aware of his own sinfulness. The same thing happened when Jesus miraculously healed a man possessed with a legion of demons. Rather than having this great man of God join their village, the people pleaded with Jesus to leave. It's humbling to meet God. But when you meet him, you change.

My friend Ken always prays on his knees. Some people kid him about being "so holy," but Ken always responds, "No, I'm not holy. But believe me, if Jesus walked into this room, we wouldn't be sitting around on chairs. We'd be spread out on the floor in fear. So when I pray, that's exactly what happens. When I pray, I'm in the presence of the Lord, and I want to be face down before Him."

In recognizing who you are in Christ, you can look upon others with new eyes. My perspective of other people changed dramatically when I became a Christian. Rather than seeing people as tools to use, I began to see them as people to love. And by seeing them with Christ's eyes, you no longer are stuck measuring people by the world's standards.

For example, some of the great men and women of God haven't been huge successes in their vocations. Paul was a tentmaker, but he was used by God to preach the gospel before kings. Peter was a fisherman, but he became the spokesman for the early church. Matthew was a tax collector, but he wrote the book that has brought more Jews to a saving knowledge of their Messiah than any other text. Sometimes the great soldiers of God aren't so famous in the world.

I once discipled a guy who always came late. He was one of those easy-going guys, with hardly a care in the world. He wasn't a winner in the world's eyes. He'd never really had much success in his career. I began to think I was wasting my time. Then one day he said to me, "Oh, by the way, Phil, I talked to that lawyer in your firm."

I stopped dead in my tracks. "Charlie? Charlie Phillips? You talked to Charlie Phillips?" My mind was racing. I'd been trying for two years to talk with Charlie Phillips, a top lawyer in my firm. He'd never been able to open up with me. I hadn't gotten to first base with him, and I was afraid this guy might have made a bad impression and blown all the work I'd been trying to do.

"Yeah," he said with shrug. "I led him to the Lord."

"Wait a minute," I said, picking my jaw up off the floor. "You led Charlie Phillips to the Lord?"

"Uh-huh."

"Charlie Phillips the lawyer?" I asked, still not believing it was possible. "The one who works in my firm?"

"Yeah. I just started talking about my faith, and he opened right up. We have a lot in common. It's like we just clicked, you know?"

I couldn't believe it. Two years I'd spent working on this lawyer, with nothing to show for it, and in two minutes this guy had him praying the sinner's prayer. It was a humbling experience, and I learned once again to see people through Christ's eyes, to look upon the heart. I had once again judged a man by my own pride and prejudices. This guy might not have been a fast-track business winner at this point in his career, but he was a great soul-winner because he had a heart for people.

I've found that I grow more during a humbling situation than a glorifying situation, probably because that's when I have to lean on God rather than on my own strength. When you consider the great men of our history, they have all experienced humbling circumstances. Abraham Lincoln was undoubtedly our greatest president, but he won election with barely forty percent of the popular vote. He had lost every election he'd ever been in until that time. He wasn't even expected to be his party's nominee; he was a compromise candidate—"everybody's second choice." The day he won the election there were thirty-three states. By the time he took office, there were only twenty-seven states. After the first two years of the Civil War, Lincoln was disliked by much of his own cabinet and considered a sure loser in his reelection bid. But all that losing helped shape a great man, with a vision not only for victory, but for restoring the pride of the nation.

Moses had to go through the humbling experience of herding sheep to learn to be a great leader. Job had to go through the humbling circumstances of losing everything. The nation of Israel had to experience forty humbling years of wandering in the wilderness for not obeying the Lord. In every case, it made the people stronger.

Joseph had perhaps the most humbling experience of all. He didn't deserve to be sold into slavery. He didn't deserve to be falsely accused of sexual harassment. He didn't deserve to be in prison, nor did he deserve to be ignored by the man he helped. But God worked in all those situations to prepare him and make him strong. Joseph came out of prison a far different man than he went in. And he didn't blame his brothers, isolate himself, or become a hard man. Instead he learned the lesson of humility, and cared for the needs of the people. He was even able to say to his brothers, "Am I in the place of God?

You intended to harm me, but God intended it for good, to accomplish what is now being done: the saving of many lives" (Genesis 50:19-20). Joseph went on to be used by God to save a starving world. That's our call, too, to save a starving world hungry for God.

What a wonderful perspective! All the humbling circumstances had come from God, and had been for a purpose—to save lives. All those bad experiences you've had—they didn't happen by accident. They were events with a purpose. God was shaping you, and His eventual goal was to save lives. He wants to make you into the kind of soldier who brings other people into the kingdom. Don't be ashamed of your circumstances—look for the way God is going to use them for His good.

I've had my share of humbling experiences, and I'm sure the Lord brings them about to help me grow. The first time I ever met the Board of Directors at CBMC, we all piled into my van so I could drive everyone to a meeting. I ran out of gas on the way, with all those prominent professional men sitting in my car. One time I took my daughter Abigail with me on a trip, I made sure to explain to her all the things I'd learned as an "experienced traveller." Except we were going to Jamaica, and I forgot to bring my passport. I've learned the importance of being humble, especially if I'm going to make a lot of mistakes!

The fact is, we all should be humble. We all deserve the cross. God owes nothing to any of us; He offers us life out of His boundless mercy and love. We have a tendency to talk about rights, but we have no rights before God. All the lawyers are going to be arguing with God about the injustice of hell when they're at the judgment seat, but the fact is we all deserve hell. There is none that is righteous. No one has earned his way into heaven. If I can remember each day that I deserve the cross, and that anything good that comes out of my ministry is because of the power and blessing of God, I'll have a good day.

When you became a soldier in the army of God, you stopped thinking about just yourself. Servants are trustworthy with the interests of others. Paul, writing to the Philippian Christians, said these words about his friend Timothy: "I hope in the Lord Jesus to send Timothy to you soon, that I also may be cheered when I receive news about you. I have no one else like him, who takes a genuine interest in your welfare. For everyone looks out for his own interests, not those of Jesus Christ. But you know that Timothy has proved himself, because as a son with his father he has served with me in the work of the gospel" (Philippians 2:19-22).

Did you know that there are people watching you? No matter who you are, if you are a Christian then people are watching. Your family is watching. Your co-workers are watching. Your neighbors are watching. They want to know if Christ is making a noticeable difference in your life, so that they can trust you with their concerns the way the Philippians trusted Timothy. They want to see if you are humble and interested in their lives, or selfish and interested in your own. Timothy looked after the interests of Jesus Christ. He knew it was his responsibility to share Christ with everyone, and to reveal God's love by looking after the needs of others.

I think the entire premise of discipleship is based upon humility. It's all about giving your life away. It's about considering the eternal situation of someone else and wanting to make it better. To be a servant, to be tender, requires humility.

Soldiers, be humble with those around you. Follow the example of Christ and tenderly care for the needs of others. There is nothing feminine or unmanly about loving people. Reveal your tender side to others, so that they can get to know your heart.

CHAPTER TWENTY

Willing to Suffer

I t's hard work being a soldier. Every soldier in battle knows that he is in harm's way, and the possibility exists that he will be wounded. Suffering comes with soldiering. The people who follow Christ are going to suffer.

Peter, one of the great soldiers of Christendom, told the early church, "Do not be surprised at the painful trial you are suffering, as though something strange were happening to you. But rejoice that you participate in the sufferings of Christ, so that you may be overjoyed when his glory is revealed. If you are insulted because of the name of Christ, you are blessed, for the Spirit of glory and of God rests on you" (1 Peter 4:12-14).

You belong to God, but the world belongs to Satan. The world hates God and wants to strike at Him, so it hates you because you are His. Suffering shouldn't surprise us. We're at war—that's what happens in a war. We should be more surprised if we don't suffer. When you suffer for the cause of Christ, you are given a special blessing from God.

Paul once told Timothy, "Everyone who wants to live a godly life in Christ Jesus will be persecuted" (2 Timothy 3:12). It's bound to happen. Standing for your faith is a difficult task. So Peter says we ought to rejoice in suffering. We ought to take suffering as a sign that we are on the right team—Satan isn't going to bother with people who are doing nothing! The people who have accomplished more for God have been targeted by Satan for special attack. Martin Luther once sensed the presence of the devil so close at hand he threw an ink well at him. When you are serving the Lord effectively, you are attracting the devil's attention.

However, Peter goes on to warn us about suffering because of our own mistakes: "If you suffer, it should not be as a murderer or thief or any other kind of criminal, or even as a meddler" (1 Peter 4:15). King David suffered, but it was largely because of his own mistakes. Sin brings suffering to the Christian. Sin kept Joshua's armies from taking Ai, it put Samson in bondage, and it put Jonah in the belly of the whale. God won't allow you to live your life in sin if you are living for Him. He will allow you to suffer the consequences, in hopes of turning you around. After David had sinned with Bathsheba, then had her husband killed, he experienced suffering. "Have mercy on me, O God, according to your unfailing love," David prayed, "according to your great compassion blot out my iniquity and cleanse me from my sin. For I know my transgressions, and my sin is always before me" (Psalm 51:1-3). Sin had created a barrier between David and his God, and David didn't want to live with that barrier. He needed to be in a right relationship with the Lord.

If you are suffering from the consequences of your sin, confess it to the Lord, accept the result, and move on. You're going to have to live with the results. David lived with the results of his sin with Bathsheba for the rest of his life. Sometimes we just have to accept the fact that we are sinners saved by grace.

A friend of mine was in leadership at a ministry when his unmarried daughter became pregnant. He wanted to quit in shame, but was encouraged to stay and work with people in crisis. Now he can better understand the hurt others are going through, and God is using him in great ways to minister to people.

Of course, sometimes we suffer for no apparent reason. Job lost everything he had—home, possessions, even his family—and he never really knew why. He asked the Lord why so many calamities had befallen him, but the only answer he got from God was, "Trust me. I know what I'm doing." Sometimes it is the plan of God to allow Christians to suffer for His greater purpose, of which we may never be aware.

A man in ministry was in a terrible automobile accident. It was a fluke thing—he was driving his family on the freeway when a part fell off a truck and pierced his car's gas tank. All six of his children burned to death in their car. That father and mother suffered greatly, but their faith in God is amazing. They forgave. They still believe in a God who has a plan. The father has continued in ministry. This couple's faith is inspiring. Thousands of people who heard about this unbelievable loss gained a greater view of God by watching them deal with their pain with a godly view of life.

One of my favorite hymns has a great story behind it. In the mid-1800's, the daughters of a pastor, Horatio Spafford, were drowned when their ship went down in the middle of a trans-Atlantic crossing. Spafford learned about the tragedy when he received a telegram from his wife that read, "All lost, save one." Crushed, Spafford insisted on finding the spot where they were lost so that he could throw a wreath onto the waters. Sailing by himself, he asked the captain of the ship to notify him when they approached the location of the tragedy. When he was told they were in the general vicinity of that lost ship, it was too foggy for him to see anything. He stood on deck, looking out into the mist of the sea, crying. Then he went back to his stateroom and wrote great words of faith: "When peace, like a river, attendeth my way; when sorrows like sea billows roll—whatever my lot, thou hast taught me to say, 'It is well, it is well with my soul.' Though Satan should buffet, though trials should come, let this blest assurance control: That Christ has regarded my helpless estate and hath shed his own blood for my soul. It is well with my soul. It is well, it is well with my soul."

I don't know why the righteous suffer. I don't understand why the innocent suffer. That is the question of the ages. Perhaps it is only to contrast the differences between the lost and the people of God. When an unsaved person develops terminal cancer, he has no hope for a better existence. But in contrast, the saved person has a solid hope in an eternity where there is no more gloom or sorrow or sickness or death. Perhaps the Lord allows Christians to suffer so that the world can see the difference in how they handle pain. But I do know that God has a plan. Things don't happen to Christians by accident. The Lord uses events to bring about His will, even when we cannot understand them.

My spiritual great-great-grandparents, Joe and Gladys, have modeled the life in Christ for many years. Through a series of tragedies they showed us how to handle suffering and death. I was with Joe in a meeting when he received the phone call telling him that his son-in-law was suffering from an aggressive form of brain cancer, from which he soon died. To watch this family go through such pain was horrible. Yet at the same time, it was wonderful because they modeled faithfulness in suffering and obedience in tragedy. Shortly after, Gladys went through a long period of debilitating cancer, and we saw in Joe how suffering could produce humility. To see Joe walk through the double dose of pain was almost more than I could bear. We all lost two great members of our spiritual family. Gladys had mothered all of us, and now she is gone from us but alive in heaven.

Not long after Gladys died, Joe told me that the Lord was teaching him the deeper meaning of all those verses he had memorized about trusting God. He said, "Phil, when these things happen, you've got a choice. You can let God break you, laying yourself on His altar and allowing His masterful hand to teach you deeply and make you like the Lord Jesus Christ, or you can resist, blame, resent and withdraw from Him. One choice produces humility; the other produces bitterness." Joe not only taught us all how to lead people to Christ, walk as Christians and disciple others. He also taught us how to give up one another to the Lord. I've always loved being around Joe, but now there is even a sweeter fragrance of our Lord—that aroma of a life sacrificed for our Savior.

One thing that has become clear to me is that people in our world want to know what's going to happen. On the mountain on which I live, there is a set of sharp curves in the road that resemble the letter "W." People always slow way down when they come to those curves. They don't know what's ahead. Sometimes that's what Christians can be—guides for those who need help on the path.

A friend of mine, a successful businessman, counsels young men who are just getting started. He calls himself a "guide," and he says that his ministry "is just to help young entrepreneurs read the road-map of life." Some experienced soldiers are there just to help the new soldiers learn to survive.

As a Christian, you can expect to suffer. 1 Peter 4 goes on to say, "If you suffer as a Christian, do not be ashamed, but praise God that you bear that name. For it is time for judgment to begin with the family of God; and if it begins with us, what will the outcome be for those who do not obey the gospel of God? And if it is hard for the righteous to be saved, what will become of the ungodly and the sinner? So then, those who suffer according to God's will should commit themselves to their faithful Creator and continue to do good" (vv. 16-19).

If you suffer for your commitment to Christ, don't feel ashamed. Paul wasn't ashamed of his chains, though he never liked them. Peter wasn't ashamed of being beaten, though I'm sure he hated every minute of it. John wasn't ashamed to be exiled to Patmos, though he would rather have been with his friends at Ephesus. They all suffered for the name of Jesus. The world was trying to strike out at God, and those dedicated soldiers were the handiest targets. So it is with you. Peter tells us not to be ashamed, but instead to praise God for being so evident in your life. If Satan can see Christ in you, he and his demons will tremble, for they know they cannot defeat the power of God. You have the holy power of the Lord Almighty at your disposal. The Spirit lives inside of you. Others should be able to see Him at work through your life. You may get hurt when they lash out at God, but don't let that surprise you. Take it as part of the hazard of war.

When my son Paul was first starting to play city-league baseball, he once took a bad bounce off his forehead. It hurt him, but he stayed in and played. Other players on the team took courage that this new kid could get hurt and remain in the game. It's the same in wartime. Other people will be watching you, and if they see you quit as soon as something painful comes along, they'll want to quit too. Your life influences others. But by the same token, if they see you get hurt and keep playing, they'll take courage and want to keep playing too. Those on the sideline may actually develop the courage to get in the game.

While I was in Viet Nam, I was part of Operation Essex, an offensive against the North Vietnamese forces. I fought for hours on end, until I didn't have anything left to fight with. I was completely exhausted, lying on the ground next to a friend of mine, when the request came for volunteers to go pick up the wounded. I thought I was too tired to answer the call, so I just lay there. But the guy next to me got up and volunteered to bring back the casualties. He went out that day and won the Navy Cross for bravery. I think back on that day and wonder what would have happened if I had answered the call. Was I really so spent that I could not have gone?

Christ is calling you to suffer. It isn't going to be pleasant, but it's required for those who are going to accomplish anything important. If you really want to do battle with Satan, you may as well plan to suffer. Though it will hurt, Christ has promised that you will survive.

A missionary doctor, who had spent forty years of his life ministering in the primitive villages of Africa, finally decided to retire and come home. He wired ahead that he would be returning by ship, and gave the date and time of his arrival. As he crossed the Atlantic, he thought back over all the years he had spent helping to heal the people of Africa, both physically and spiritually. Then his thoughts raced forward, to the grand homecoming he knew awaited him in the America he had left so many years earlier.

As that ship pulled into port, his heart swelled with pride as he saw the huge homecoming that had been prepared in his honor. A great crowd of people had gathered, and had hung a "Welcome Home" banner across the front of the terminal. But as that doctor stepped out onto the dock, no one burst into applause. His heart sank. These people had not come for him, but for a movie star who had also been aboard the ship. He waited for hours, but no one showed up to meet him. His heart breaking, he looked heavenward and asked, "Lord, was it too much to ask that someone be here to welcome me home?" Then, in the quietness of his heart, he felt the Lord reply, "You're not home yet. When you get home to me, you will be welcomed." That missionary had suffered in another culture, and was suffering at the lack of attention paid him on his return. But he was comforted that one day all suffering would cease.

In Revelation, chapters two and three, Christ brings a message to each of the churches of Asia Minor. Of those seven, there is only one church to which the Lord offers no rebuke. The church at Smyrna is commended for its strength under suffering. They have suffered persecution, poverty, slander, and affliction. Christ's message for them is simple: "Be faithful." Even in the midst of persecution, be faithful. Our culture would prefer that His message was something different, like a promise to end the suffering, or an explanation that one day they will know why they have suffered. The Lord offers none of that, but only a call for them to continue in their faithful suffering.

Sometimes we'll suffer as soldiers. Nobody likes to hear that, but if I neglected to say it, I wouldn't be offering the whole truth. If you live for Jesus in this world, you can expect to suffer the way Jesus suffered. If you want to be a soldier, you might as well decide right now to endure it.

CHAPTER TWENTY-ONE

Taking Others into Combat

I f you're going to be a soldier, you're going to have to take
others into battle with you. There are unsaved people out
there, waiting to hear the Good News and join the army of
God. There are baby Christians who don't even know there is
a war going on, and they need strong leaders who can take
them onto the battlefield and set an example for them to follow. And there are mature soldiers who just need somebody to
fight alongside, so that they don't feel they are in the war by
themselves. The soldiers in the army of God can change the
world, if they'll only fight for God's purposes with God's
power.

For them to do so, they have to have godly leaders. Christ is the head of the church, and He has put holy people in charge of the battle. The Lord has arranged for men of valor and wisdom to offer direction to others. Their responsibility is to coordinate, facilitate, and develop the soldiers, so that we work together for Christ to make disciples.

The Battle of Shiloh, fought in April 1862, was the first great fight of the Civil War. It was spring, so the trees were full of leaves, making it hard to know north from south, and the roads were nothing more than meandering cowpaths. None of the men had ever seen combat before. The soldiers didn't know about hand-to-hand combat until the enemy charged their lines. The generals didn't know how to manage a great mass of men during the confusion of a battle. One hundred thousand men went into a great, chaotic mess. Since no one knew their job, the losses were enormous. At the end of the day, more than twenty percent of the men involved lay dead or wounded on the field. In those early days, the North had a huge advantage in arms and material. If they'd had the leadership, most experts agree the Civil War would have been much shorter. But without the leaders, the army suffered.

God's army is in desperate need of leaders, particularly servant leaders who look to the interests of Jesus Christ rather than their own. That's why Paul took such great care to explain in his letters what the leaders of the church should be like. "Since an overseer is entrusted with God's work, he must be blameless—not overbearing, not quick-tempered, not given to much wine, not violent, not pursuing dishonest gain. Rather, he must be hospitable, one who loves what is good, who is self-controlled, upright, holy and disciplined. He must hold firmly to the trustworthy message as it has been taught, so that he can encourage others by sound doctrine and refute those who oppose it" (Titus 1:7-9). If the leaders remain close to Christ, so will the army. As servants, we've got to be equipping and training those who can become leaders.

Those who would be soldiers must also have a vision. That battle I just mentioned, fought near Shiloh, is a good example of unity. The Southern soldiers felt they were fighting to protect their land and their rights, while the leaders of the Northern soldiers had a much more difficult task. President Lincoln and his generals had to unify their soldiers, but they had to do it around the larger, more obtuse goals of preserving the Union and freeing the slaves. It took longer to unify the Northern troops, but when they did, they rallied everyone to the cause.

A vision is a powerful tool for people at war. Churchill rallied an uninvolved country to fight a fascist terror. George Washington and other Revolutionary leaders rallied a divided populace to the cause of freedom. Peter grew a small band of disciples in Jerusalem into a mighty church of more than three thousand by offering the vision of Christ as the prophesied Messiah. As servants we must be sharing the vision with people, so that they understand about the spiritual war.

Developing a Battle Plan

If we're going to lead others into battle, we also have to have a disciple-making plan. We've got to evangelize our communities, and help people share their faith so that they are reproducing themselves into the lives of others. Then we've got to disciple those people into maturity. As mature believers, we are responsible to care for newborn spiritual babies. We've got to teach truth, model it, and tenderly encourage others to foster obedience to the truth in their own lives. This is all done with the aim of producing more soldiers, because if the army of God does not have active, ministering soldiers, it will never accomplish anything of importance. We've got to show other soldiers a tender concern, offering a mutual and intense caring for those struggling with the pressures of combat. Too many churches are full of spectators—noncombatants at a time when we need to be promoting one another to love and good works. We've got to get people onto the battle lines.

Soldiers in Time of Need

Finally, if we are going to take people into combat we must be praying. If you want to shake the world, you're going to have to release the power of God through prayer. A sinful world is only moved toward God as the church is moved of God. Satan wants you too busy to pray, so the first step in defeating him is to get on your knees and repent of your prayerlessness. Cleanse your soul and begin praying for the cleansing of others. The devil wants you to go to hell, but if you're already saved he wants you to have a shallow, uneventful life in the Lord. The church is filled with Christians who have deep knowledge but shallow practice, physical strength but spiritual weakness, worldly wealth but spiritual poverty, and religious piety but spiritual carnality. You see, God changes men, not things. He breaks chains, expels demons, rescues cities, stops Satan, and brings revival to a lost world. Pray and you begin to change the world.

God is calling you to be a soldier in a time of great need. The world is in chaos, and you can bring peace. People's lives are in turmoil, and you have the solution. You can bring freedom to those in bondage, joy to those in complaint, and meaning to those seeking purpose. You have the opportunity to share the love of God with lost souls, and usher them into the kingdom.

As I've said before, people are watching you. They have been looking around to see whose life is different, and they are watching you closely, to see if your God really makes a difference. You have a responsibility to share Christ with them.

God is good. He loves us, redeems us, and has a plan for our lives. He understands us, gives each person unique gifts, and offers us a chance to practice our gifts. He allows us to be

His emissaries on earth, and He plans to have us reign with Him in eternity.

In God's economy, there is no recession. In His truth, there is no lapse of memory. His Word is secure; it never fails. He has promised you that you will be with Him one day. God has forgiven you of your sins, having removed them as far as the east is from the west, and having paid the debt for the penalty of your sins. Even though the Lord has total knowledge, He has chosen to forget your sin. The presence of the Son, the perfection of the Father, and the power of the Spirit are all present in your life.

When you choose to tell someone about the Lord, you do so out of gratitude, not obligation. Your love for God and for others compels you to share. You're a soldier, but you have volunteered for active duty. No one forced you to join. You signed up because you believed in the cause, and that cause has changed your life.

Loving God and Loving People

Not only do you love God, you also love people. You have a heart for others, and you can't stand the thought that they are going to spend an eternity apart from God. So you tell them about the Lord, and you reveal how He has changed your life.

For two years I told my father about Christ, but he never believed. Then one day he committed suicide. I don't know if my sharing with him ever made any difference. He never told me about the three times he got fired, so I never told him about my own failures, and I wonder now if that would have made any difference. I ask myself if by explaining about what went wrong in my life and how I had dealt with it, I would have connected with him. Perhaps my own tenderness would have stirred something in his heart. I'll never know if it would have made any difference—but I am sure that God is in control of my father's situation, just as He is in control of mine and my children's. For you see, God allowed some good to result from my dad's suicide. Through it He taught me about taking others into combat.

Through my father's suicide, I have developed a burning desire to reach men for Jesus Christ; to help them be godly and faithful husbands and fathers; and to disciple men and couples to be spiritual reproducers. I want to touch the heart of that businessman who is giving his life to something that is not going to last. He's at work when his kids are at home, at the club when his wife is in need, and in the office because his relationships with his family make him feel like a failure. I want to help him wrap himself around the only One worth committing his life to. I want to help build men and women who are faithful to the interests of Jesus Christ, and concerned about the welfare of people. I want to participate in developing soldiers who have tender hearts, serving others' needs with the love of Jesus.

A friend of mine was at the funeral of an older gentleman in his church, and he tells me that during the service, the deceased's wife got up and said, "When I looked at my husband, I saw Jesus Christ." Now that's a testimony! Imagine having the person closest to you say that you reminded them of the Lord. That man must have been a wonderful servant, tenderly caring for the needs of others.

I was reading about a missionary who went to work with an Indian tribe in South America. He served them, worked with them, cared for their sick, and ministered in every way possible. After two years an older man in the village said to him, "I'm interested in this Jesus you speak about. What is he like?"

The missionary, looking him in the eye, simply said, "He's like me."

I long to be like that missionary. I want to be a tender servant, showing so much love to others that they can see Christ in me. And I want to take them into battle with me.

People are watching. They're waiting to see what my God is like, and how He works in me. Not only that, but Christians who have already met Christ are watching, waiting for someone to lead them. Inexperienced soldiers want somebody else to go first, so that they have an example to follow. They also need a tender servant to encourage them and help them succeed.

Your children are watching you. They want to see if this faith you profess really changes your life, or if it merely intrudes on your Sunday morning schedule. You are discipling your children at all times, whether you plan to or not. I heard a man speak recently about driving his kids to school. It seems his office was close to his children's school, so he drove the kids each day and dropped them off. One day he didn't go in to his office, so his wife took the kids to school. As she was driving down the highway, her six-year-old said to her, "Mommy, where are all the jerks today?" That one comment changed that man's attitude every morning. His goal is not to get down the road as quickly as possible, but to begin his day by showing his children the love and tenderness of Jesus Christ.

My oldest child, Abigail, was talking about careers with her mother. As Susy listed various ideas for her, Abigail kept shaking her head. Finally my daughter blurted out, "I want to be a physician's assistant, but someday I want to be just like you, Mom." Amen to that. Susy has been able to express her faith and achieve her ministry through our family, and it has allowed us to begin a godly legacy. Her tender love and caring service to us have helped bind us together, so that my family is a soul-winning team; a fighting squadron in the army of God.

Nobody goes into battle alone for very long. Take some others with you, and help them grow into mature soldiers like yourself.

CHAPTER TWENTY-TWO

The Battle Cry

I've replayed the scene in my mind a million times. My friend John has my machine gun. We're charging down a path. I'm the leader, and John is right behind me. We turn left, and shots ring out. I fall into the path, and John's body falls on top of me. All the bullets except the one that harmlessly went through my pack went into John's back. His body shielded me from harm. He was dead before he hit the ground.

I've asked myself over and over again, "What if I had gone right instead of left? Would it have made a difference?" I'll probably never know.

When I became a believer, my life changed. My sins were forgiven; God was in control. He loves me. He has made me strong, so that I can lead others into battle. He has made me brave, so that I can be an example to others. He has even made me tender, so that I can be a servant and minister to the needs of those around me. But I still have free choice and the ability to go the wrong way in this life.

I don't want to make mistakes. I don't ever want to fall on the wrong part of the path, to have the men following me die because of my stupidity. I don't want to leave my family exposed to Satan's attack, nor do I want to allow the men of the Christian Business Men's Committee of USA left to the devil's devices.

Instead, I want to follow Jesus Christ faithfully. I want to be trustworthy, to have a heart for people. May all my thoughts, words, and deeds share Christ. I don't want anybody to know me and not hear about Jesus. I'm a soldier now, and I've got one focus for my life. I'm going into battle, and I plan to rescue as many people out of Satan's world as possible and disciple others to do the same. My prayer is that you'll join me in the battle.

The world needs men who are brave, strong, and tender. But you can only find men like that in the army of God. Are you ready to be a soldier?

BRAVE, STRONG AND TENDER

SMALL GROUP BIBLE STUDY QUESTIONS

By
Phil Downer

with
Chip MacGregor

To order additional copies of Brave, Strong & Tender, other evangelism and discipleship ministry tools or for further information, call the CBMC order line at 1-800-566-2262

Chapter 1 - The Christian Soldier

"Christians, it's time to put on the full armor of God."

1. When do you feel like you are in a spiritual battle?

2. As you consider your current walk with God, are you more like a courageous Paul or a fearful Timothy? Why?

3. How does Satan attack you?

4. What would you say are the prime motivators in your life? What drives you?

5. As you evaluate your preparation for battle, where do you need to change your life?

For our struggle is not against flesh and blood, but against the rulers, against the authorities, against the powers of this dark world and against the spiritual forces of evil in the heavenly realms. Ephesians 6:12 (NIV)

For our struggle is not against flesh and blood, but against the rulers, against the powers, against the world forces of this darkness, against the spiritual forces of wickedness in the heavenly places. (NASV)

Chapter 2 - How to be Strong

"First, you have to acknowledge your weakness is usable by God."

1. How would you describe a strong Christian?

2. How is being strong in grace different from being strong in the world?

3. What did Timothy do to become strong?

4. Where are you weak? Where are you strong?

5. How can you exercise your spiritual strength?

"My grace is sufficient for you, for my power is made perfect in weakness." Therefore, I will boast all the more gladly about my weaknesses, so that Christ's power may rest on me. That is why, for Christ's sake, I delight in weaknesses, in insults, in hardships, in persecutions, in difficulties. For when I am weak, then I am strong. 2 Corinthians 12:9–10 (NIV)

"My grace is sufficient for you, for power is perfected in weakness." Most gladly, therefore, I will rather boast about my weaknesses, that the power of Christ may dwell in me. Therefore I am well content with weaknesses, with insults, with distresses, with persecutions, with difficulties, for Christ's sake; for when I am weak, then I am strong. (NASV)

Chapter 3 - Take Courage

"No soldier lives in fear and is effective in battle."

1. Where do you struggle in trusting God?

2. How much time do you spend in the Word? How much time would you like to spend? What would need to happen for you to reach your goal?

3. In what areas of your life do you believe you are open to attack?

4. Have you reached a place in your spiritual journey where you know you are saved? Explain your answer.

5. What fears do you have from which you desire release by the Lord?

Do not be anxious about anything, but in everything, by prayer and petition, with thanksgiving, present your requests to God. And the peace of God, which transcends all understanding, will guard your hearts and your minds in Christ Jesus. Philippians 4:6–7 (NIV)

Be anxious for nothing, but in everything by prayer and supplication with thanksgiving let your requests be made known to God. And the peace of God, which surpasses all comprehension, shall guard your hearts and your minds in Christ Jesus. (NASV)

Chapter 4 - Developing the Spirit of Power

"We can't perform miracles, but we all have the power to impact a life for Him."

1. Who is the most powerful person you know? What makes him that way?

2. Why do men seek power?

3. How can a Christian be both powerful and a slave?

4. Who are the people your life influences?

5. With whom are you actively talking about your faith? With whom would you most like to talk about your faith?

I pray that you may be active in sharing your faith, so that you will have a full understanding of every good thing we have in Christ. Philemon 1:6 (NIV)

And I pray that the fellowship of your faith may become effective through the knowledge of every good thing which is in you for Christ's sake. (NASV)

Chapter 5 - The Loving Leader - Part One

"Christ's Leadership was marked by His love for us—so much so He was willing to lay down His life on our behalf."

1. How is a leader known by his love?

2. On a scale of 1 to 10, how patient are you? What needs to happen for you to improve by two points on your scale?

3. Do you have a heart for other people? If so, how do you express it? If not, what do you need to do to develop that heart?

4. In what way does the voluntary surrender of your rights reveal your love?

5. How can a Christian be confident without being boastful?

It always protects, always trusts, always hopes, always perseveres. Love never fails. But where there are prophecies, they will cease; where there are tongues, they will be stilled; where there is knowledge, it will pass away. 1 Corinthians 13:7–9 (NIV)

Bears all things, believes all things, hopes all things, endures all things. Love never fails; but if there are gifts of prophecy, they will be done away; if there are tongues, they will cease; if there is knowledge, it will be done away. (NASV)

Chapter 6 - The Loving Leader - Part Two

"A leader too much concerned for his own welfare can never enjoy the confidence of those around him."

1. How do you commonly respond to failure?

2. In 1 Peter 3:9, we are told to respond to insult with blessing. What can a Christian do to be able to put that verse into practice?

3. In the last week, how have you used your mouth to build up those closest to you?

4. In the last thirty days, what positive investment have you made in the lives of your wife, children, co-workers, and friends? Have you done anything that they will remember one year from now?

5. As you look at Philippians 2:5–11, what example of unselfishness did Christ set for us? What is one practical step you can take to follow His example?

Do nothing out of selfish ambition or vain conceit, but in humility consider others better than yourselves. Each of you should look not only to your own interests, but also to the interests of others. Philippians 2:3–4 (NIV)

Do nothing from selfishness or empty conceit, but with humility of mind let each of you regard one another as more important than himself; do not merely look out for your own personal interests, but also for the interests of others. (NASV)

Chapter 7 - Self-Controlled Soldier

"A person who has self-control is able to restrain or give direction to his desires, actions and emotions."

1. Where do you struggle with your self-control?

2. What steps have you taken to exercise control over your challenges with lust, eating and exercise habits? What steps would help you take better control?

3. If someone were to look at your checkbook and credit card receipts, would they say you are experiencing control over your spending? Explain your answer.

4. What does it mean to "store up treasures in heaven?" How are you doing that?

5. How can a man start each day thinking about the Lord, rather than his own selfish desires?

Like a city whose walls are broken down is a man who lacks self-control. Proverbs 25:28 (NIV)

Like a city that is broken into and without walls is a man who has no control over his spirit. (NASV)

Chapter 8 - Loyal to the Cause

"Every soldier has something that's important, a line in the sand that he draws...willing to die for the cause if he has to."

1. What are you willing to die for?

2. Do you think it is fair to say that you can spot a Christian by looking at his life?

3. What principle do you derive from 1 John 1:6–7? How well are you putting that into practice?

4. In your Christian walk and ministry, do you feel like you are part of a team? Why or why not?

5. How does our love for one another reveal that we belong to Christ?

This is how we know what love is: Jesus Christ laid down his life for us. And we ought to lay down our lives for our brothers. 1 John 3:16 (NIV)

We know love by this, that He laid down His life for us; and we ought to lay down our lives for the brethren. (NASV)

Chapter 9 - The Importance of Encouragement

"Words are powerful tools, and a good soldier knows how to use them to encourage others, building them up as opposed to tearing them down."

1. In what way is a soldier a model?

2. What is the nicest compliment you ever received? Why do you appreciate it so much?

3. At what times do you struggle with unwholesome talk coming from your mouth?

4. Who needs your comfort, encouragement, and instruction?

5. What are two things you can do to begin using your words to build up others?

Do not let any unwholesome talk come out of your mouths, but only what is helpful for building others up according to their needs, that it may benefit those who listen. Ephesians 4:29 (NIV)

Let no unwholesome word proceed from your mouth, but only such a word as is good for edification according to the need of the moment, that it may give grace to those who hear. (NASV)

Chapter 10 - The Trustworthy Soldier

"Discipleship is more than a course, and mentoring more than a discussion of one's career. They both refer to a mutual relationship whereby a more mature person helps a protégé grow and develop as a disciple maker."

1. How would you define the word "trustworthy"?

2. Who is the most trustworthy person you have ever known?

3. To this point in your life, who has been your most significant mentor?

4. What difference would it have made to you if you would have had a wise, experienced mentor when you were twenty years old? (Or, if you did have a mentor, how did that relationship benefit your life?)

5. Who could benefit from your wisdom and experience?

But we proved to be gentle among you, as a nursing mother tenderly cares for her own children. Having thus a fond affection for you, we were well-pleased to impart to you not only the gospel of God but also our own lives, because you had become very dear to us. 1 Thessalonians 2:7–8 (NIV)

But we proved to be gentle among you, as a nursing mother tenderly cares for her own children. Having thus a fond affection for you, we were well-pleased to impart to you not only the gospel of God but also our own lives, because you had become very dear to us. (NASV)

Chapter 11 - Faithful in All Things

"God hasn't called me to be successful; He's called me to be faithful. It's God who determines what 'success' is."

1. Why is it important to have a man prove his faithfulness?

2. What "talents" has the Lord entrusted to you, and how are you using them?

3. What is your vision?

4. What does your lifestyle evidence as your passion?

5. Would those closest to you consider you as a man of integrity?

Do not become weary in doing good, for at the proper time we will reap a harvest if we do not give up. Galatians 6:9 (NIV)

And let us not lose heart in doing good, for in due time we shall reap if we do not grow weary. (NASV)

Chapter 12 - Teaching and Being Teachable

"The best way teacher is one who never stops being a leaven."

1. Why is it important for a soldier to be able to teach others?

2. On a scale of 1 to 10, how comfortable are you sharing your testimony with a non-Christian?

3. When was the last time you shared your faith with a non-believing friend? What were the circumstances? What was the response?

4. Who are you training in the principles of soldiering? Who would you like to be training?

5. How can you spot a person who is teachable?

And the things you have heard from me in the presence of many witnesses, these entrust to faithful men who will be able to teach others also. 2 Timothy 2:2 (NIV)

And the things which you have heard from me in the presence of many witnesses, these entrust to faithful men, who will be able to teach others also. (NASV)

Chapter 13 - No Rest for the Weary

"Being a Christian soldier is hard work, and the Lord has to shape and mold you so that you perform the perfect function He has planned for you."

1. What is the motivation of a soldier?

2. How is your Christian life like an athlete's training?

3. Where are you laboring for Jesus Christ?

4. How would you explain Matthew 10:34–39 in your own words?

5. What change needs to happen in your life if you are to become a clean vessel, "made holy, useful to the Master and prepared to do any good work" (2 Timothy 2:21)?

Endure hardship with us like a good soldier of Christ Jesus. No one serving as a soldier gets involved in civilian affairs—he wants to please his commanding officer. 2 Timothy 2:3–4 (NIV)

Suffer hardship with me, as a good soldier of Christ Jesus. No soldier in active service entangles himself in the affairs of everyday life, so that he may please the one who enlisted him as a soldier. (NASV)

Chapter 14 - Able to Handle God's Word

"In your quiet time with God you'll find that He'll offer you guidance, bring you strength, and overwhelm your troubles and concerns with peace."

1. How often do you have a quiet time? What do you do during your quiet time?

2. What are you reading in your Bible? What sort of blessing are you gaining from it?

3. What are you praying about? What was your last significant answer to prayer?

4. What does it mean to "meditate" on Scripture? How do you meditate?

5. What passages of Scripture would you most like to memorize?

Call to me and I will answer you and tell you great and unsearchable things you do not know. Jeremiah 33:3 (NIV)

Call to Me, and I will answer you, and I will tell you great and mighty things, which you do not know. (NASV)

Chapter 15 - How to Remain Pure

"If a man can guard his eyegate, so that nothing impure enters his mind, he'll protect his purity."

1. How comfortable would you be if someone dug through your secret life?

2. What steps do you take to protect your integrity?

3. Where does Satan most often attack you?

4. How can a Christian defeat the temptations of Satan?

5. What easy way out is Satan encouraging you to take? What would help make you strong to do the tough things for the Lord?

I made a covenant with my eyes not to look lustfully at a girl. Job 31:1 (NIV)

I have made a covenant with my eyes; how then could I gaze at a virgin? (NASV)

Chapter 16 - The Necessity of Obedience

"Every Christian is either living in obedience or living in rebellion."

1. In your own words, why is obedience so hard?

2. Is it demeaning to be a servant?

3. What is the hardest thing God ever called you to do? How did you respond?

4. How can a Christian be strong and obey God in the face of danger? In the face of looking foolish?

5. What does it mean in 1 Samuel 15:22 when it says, "To obey is better than sacrifice?"

But Samuel replied, "Does the LORD delight in burnt offerings and sacrifices as much as in obeying the voice of the LORD? To obey is better than sacrifice, and to heed is better than the fat of rams." 1 Samuel 15:22 (NIV)

And Samuel said, "Has the LORD as much delight in burnt offerings and sacrifices as in obeying the voice of the LORD? Behold, to obey is better than sacrifice, and to heed than the fat of rams." (NASV)

Chapter 17 - Focused on the Battle

"If you lose your focus, you can lose the battle."

1. What is the focus of your life and how does prayer fit in?

2. Who is the enemy? How can we remain convinced of that fact when we are doing battle with a spouse or co-worker?

3. What goals do you have for your family and marriage and personal quiet time with the Lord?

4. Who is on your Ten Most Wanted List, the list of ten people you want to lead to the Lord?

5. What changes do you need to make to your schedule to ensure that you are involved in leading others to Christ and discipling soldiers into maturity?

One of those days Jesus went out to a mountainside to pray, and spent the night praying to God. Luke 6:12 (NIV)

And it was at this time that He went off to the mountain to pray, and He spent the whole night in prayer to God. (NASV)

Chapter 18 - Serving Under Authority

"Christ is depending upon His army to do His work, and His army is dependent upon Him for the power to do it. We are under His authority, working as His servants in the world."

1. Who is the most committed believer you have ever met? What impresses you most about their life?

2. How is a Christian man under authority?

3. Do you find it difficult to serve under authority? Why or why not?

4. If you were Philemon, how would you have responded to Paul?

5. In what areas are you fighting with God about your obedience to His commands?

But the eyes of the LORD are on those who fear Him, on those whose hope is in his unfailing love. Psalm 33:18 (NIV)

Behold the eye of the LORD is on those who fear Him, On those who hope for His lovingkindness. (NASV)

Chapter 19 - A Servant is Humble

"We all deserve the cross."

1. What is the most humbling experience you have ever endured?

2. How does a humbling circumstance make some men hard?

3. How can a man learn to delight in God during a difficult situation?

4. Do you find yourself delighting more in God or in your work and accomplishments?

5. To become a truly tender man, what changes does the Lord need to make in your life?

This is what the LORD says, "Let not the wise man boast of his wisdom or the strong man boast of his strength or the rich man boast of his riches, but let him who boasts boast about this: that he understands and knows me, that I am the LORD, who exercises kindness, justice and righteousness on earth, for in these I delight," declares the LORD. Jeremiah 9:23–24 (NIV)

Thus says the LORD, "Let not a wise man boast of his wisdom, and let not the mighty man boast of his might, let not a rich man boast of his riches; but let him who boasts boast of this, that he understands and knows Me, that I am the LORD who exercises lovingkindness, justice, and righteousness on earth; for I delight in these things," declares the LORD. (NASV)

Chapter 20 - Able to Handle God's Word

"If you live for Jesus in this world, you can expect to suffer the way Jesus suffered."

1. Why can we expect persecution?

2. What do you say to a suffering Christian who asks you, "Why would God allow this?"

3. What does the Word of God say about how it is possible to rejoice in the face of suffering?

4. What suffering have you had to endure?

5. How did you get through it? What impact did it have on your   life?

In fact, everyone who wants to live a godly life in Christ Jesus will be persecuted. 2 Timothy 3:12 (NIV)

And indeed, all who desire to live godly in Christ Jesus will be persecuted. (NASV)

Chapter 21 - Taking Others Into Combat

"As servants, we've got to be equipping and training those who can become leaders."

1. In your own words, why is it important for God's army to have strong leaders?

2. In your life, who is watching you?

3. What are you praying for the Lord to do through you?

4. What is your disciple-making plan?

5. Who would you say is on your team? Why can't we go into the spiritual battle alone?

Since an overseer is entrusted with God's work, he must be blameless—not overbearing, not quick-tempered, not given to drunkenness, not violent, not pursuing dishonest gain. Rather he must be hospitable, one who loves what is good, who is self-controlled, upright, holy and disciplined. He must hold firmly to the trustworthy message as it has been taught, so that he can encourage others by sound doctrine and refute those who oppose it. Titus 1:7–9 (NIV)

For the overseer must be above reproach as God's steward, not self-willed, not quick-tempered, not addicted to wine, not pugnacious, not fond of sordid gain, but hospitable, loving what is good, sensible, just, devout, self-controlled, holding fast the faithful word which is in accordance with the teaching, that he may be able both to exhort in sound doctrine and to refute those who contradict. (NASV)

Chapter 22 - The Battle Cry

"I'm going into battle, and I plan to rescue as many people out of Satan's world as possible and disciple others to do the same. My prayer is that you'll join me in the battle. The world needs men and women who are brave, strong and tender."

1. How has God changed your life?

2. In what areas is He still working on changing you?

3. In one sentence, what is the purpose of your life?

4. What is left for you to do to prepare you for the battle?

5. Who are you planning to take with you?

The least of you will become a thousand, the smallest a mighty nation. I am the LORD; in its time I will do this swiftly. Isaiah 60:22 (NIV)

The smallest one will become a clan, and the least one a mighty nation. I, the LORD, will hasten it in its time. (NASV)